ᵀᴴᴱ Edward Bernays Reader

From Propaganda to The Engineering of Consent

INTRODUCTION BY NANCY SNOW

PUBLISHING

NEW YORK, NY

Ig Publishing
Box 2547
New York, NY 10163
www.igpub.com

ISBN 978-163246-204-6

CONTENTS

INTRODUCTION

THE MERRIAM-WEBSTER DICTIONARY DISTINGUISHES between two types of influencers. The first and original definition refers to "a person who inspires or guides the actions of others." The twenty-first century meaning of an influencer more often than not refers to "a person who is able to generate interest in something (such as a consumer product) by posting about it on social media." The first definition connotes exclusivity. Not everyone can be an influencer without proper training, education, and insight. The latter connotes inclusivity. Anyone can be a social media influencer with enough moxie and drive to become talked about or followed online.

Bernays was the *ursprung* influencer. There is no one who compares to him before or since he lived. His life's work, the most influential of which is presented in this book, was astonishingly ahead of its time but also seamlessly applicable to today's media and propaganda environment.

The Viennese-born Edward Louis Bernays, double nephew

of Sigmund Freud,[1] would have heartily rejected the populist concept today that anyone can be an influencer. He believed in war and peacetime propaganda campaigns that served the interests of the ruling power classes against the unreliable, undisciplined, but malleable masses. Bernays would surely have been repelled by the lowest common denominator tendencies in today's social media platforms where often the most sensationalized images get the most likes. He was a man of letters who graduated from Cornell University, part of the elite Ivy League in his adopted country, the United States.

At first glance it might appear that his 1912 degree in agriculture—he initially aspired to work in his father's grain export business—was far adrift from his future profession in press agentry, journalism, and wartime propaganda. But indeed, the verb form of the noun propaganda has agricultural origins. To propagate is to cause an organism to be fruitful and multiply by process of reproduction from the parent stock, like a farmer seeding his growing field. In the case of Bernays, he was literally the parent stock of the discipline and industry we know today as public relations. His offspring were those ideas that took flight on behalf of his clients, the foremost being the United States government during World War I. In seven short years after his graduation and the war's end in 1919, he opened an office as Public Relations Counselor in New York City. Public Relations Counselor had a much better ring to it than Government Propagandist and so began Bernays' seventy-year venture into building a client base and self-promoting his own reputation as the nation's foremost persuader and creator of overt acts through covert means. He died in 1995 at age 103.

---

1. His mother was Freud's sister. His father was the brother of Freud's wife.

While Bernays is acknowledged as pioneering the field of public relations—he's often referred to as its father or grandfather—his influence is not discussed enough in scholarly circles. The modern public relations industry doesn't seem to quite know what to do with him or his legacy since he is forever associated with the pejorative term propaganda, a concept in the United States that is almost universally reviled as lies or what only one's worst enemy engages in. Students of PR do not think of themselves as corporate propagandists and avoid association with its ancillaries like spin doctoring and hucksterism. To its credit, the Museum of Public Relations in New York City acknowledges Bernays as a pioneer in the field.

Bernays openly embraced propaganda because he believed that it worked well, with his proper guidance and counsel, to support client opinions as the public's own interests. A man who published works such as *Crystallizing Public Opinion* (1923) and *Propaganda* (1928) is a man of self-assuredness about the impact of his public opinion management on people's thinking and behavior. It's no surprise that another man of influence of Bernays' era, Henry Luce, would identify Bernays in *Life* magazine as one of the 100 most influential Americans of the twentieth century. Both men would bookend the apex of influence in the American century.

Journalist Bill Moyers interviewed Bernays for his 1983 program, "The Image Makers."[2] The then nonagenarian Bernays told Moyers that his public relations counsel was a form of good propaganda (aka "proper-ganda") and not "improper-ganda." Woodrow Wilson's Committee on Public Information (Creel Committee), for which

---

2. Bill Moyers, *The Image Makers*, "A Walk Through the 20th Century," Public Broadcasting System, April 14, 1983.

Bernays first worked, was a propaganda operation designed to persuade the masses at home and abroad that World War I would be "the war to end all wars" and would help to "make the world safe for democracy." After the war, Bernays accompanied President Wilson as a press attaché to the peace talks in Paris where he witnessed the emotional zeal that the Europeans placed on the great liberator, Wilson. When he returned to America, Bernays said, "I decided that if you could use propaganda for war, you could certainly use it for peace."

In the Flapper 1920s, Bernays hung up his sign in service to private clients, giving public relations a commercial capitalist tinge. One of his first industry clients was the Beech-nut Company, which produced bacon. It wasn't enough to devise a plan to ask war-fatigued consumers to eat more Beech-nut bacon product; Bernays wanted to be an indispensable PR counsel to the entire bacon producing industry. Just like he had during wartime with selling war for democracy, Bernays chose to associate bacon with something important in peacetime America, the ideal meat choice for the first big meal before fathers went off to work and children went off to school. Who better to shape that opinion than male doctors in white coats, who gave testimonials associating bacon with a hearty breakfast and as an excellent way to start one's day? Ordering an American-style breakfast anywhere in the world will, even today, almost always produce a plate of bacon and eggs.

American Tobacco Company president George W. Hill sought the counsel of Bernays to help him serve their growing female client base who had earned the right to vote in 1920. Unlike men, women who smoked could do so only in private as it was considered unladylike if she smoked while walking down the street. She might as well have been a street walker. Bernays chose to tear down the wall between the private and public by associating women's rights to vote with smoking. The annual Easter Parade in New York City offered an opportunity for Bernays to hire fashionable models, including his own secretary Bertha Hunt, to walk along taking drags on their "torches of freedom." The undercover Hunt signed a telegram sent to a list of New York's finest debutantes: "In the interests of equality of the sexes and to fight another sex taboo I and other young women will light another torch of freedom by smoking cigarettes while strolling on Fifth Avenue Easter Sunday." Bernays hired photographers to document his campaign. The front page of the Monday, April 1, 1929 *New York Times* read: "Group of Girls Puff at Cigarettes as a Gesture of 'Freedom.'" The article described the manufactured event: "About a dozen young women strolled back and forth between St. Thomas's and St. Patrick's while the parade was at its peak, ostentatiously smoking cigarettes. Two were asked which brand they favored and they named it. One of the group explained the cigarettes were 'torches of freedom' lighting the way to the day when women could smoke on the street as casually as men." Could the group spokeswoman have been the planted Ms. Hunt?

Within five weeks, freedom-loving female puffers were allowed access to the smoking areas of theaters, just like men. Spokespeople and sponsorship. Now that's the American way of promoting democracy! After the first Surgeon General Report in 1964 linked quitting smoking to healthy longevity, Bernays made an about face and rejected any further association with tobacco manufacturers. He could no longer advise a company whose product, when used as advertised, could kill or shorten the life of its user.

As a doctoral student of international relations at American University's School of International Service in Washington, D.C., I missed an opportunity to see Mr. Bernays in person—at the ripe old age of ninety-seven—in 1989 when he presented a founder's perspective on public relations at AU's School of Communication.[3] His interviewer, Dean Sanford Ungar, prompted Bernays to reveal one of his first political campaigns, which was to soften the dour image of Calvin Coolidge. Alice Roosevelt Longworth, daughter of Teddy, had adopted an already trafficked bon mot that Coolidge looked as if he had been weaned on a pickle.[4] The salty expression soon went national. Bernays said that the best way to combat any rumor is not with the obvious response, denial. Better to blanket the rumor with an overt act, an idea that he based on the work of his fellow Committee on Public Information member, journalist Walter Lippman. Lippman, who published *Public Opinion* (1922) eighteen months before Bernays published his first book, *Crystallizing Public Opinion*, described news as "any overt act that juts out of the routine of circumstance."

A good public relations man like Bernays advised his client to carry out some overt act in order to interrupt the continuity of life. This will bring about a response that favors the client's goals.[5] In case of Coolidge, the sourpuss president needed a personality makeover. What would a true curmudgeon weaned on a pickle never do? Invite

---

3. Edward Bernays, "Public Relations: A Founder's Perspective," American University School of Communication, January 23, 1989.
4. Robert Klose, "In era of Trump, I miss the reticence of Calvin Coolidge," *Bangor Daily News*, January 10, 2020.
5. Stuart Ewen, *PR! A Social History of Spin*. New York: Basic Books, 1996.

a group of prominent Broadway vaudevillian actors and performers like Al Jolson and the Ziegfeld Follies girls to have a pancake breakfast with him at The White House. And this is exactly what Bernays arranged for on Friday, October 17, 1924. After breakfast, the group reconvened on the White House lawn where Al Jolson sang the 1924 campaign song whose lyrics included *Coolidge is the one. Without a lot of fuss, he did a lot for us, so let's reciprocate and keep him there! He's never asleep, still water runs deep.* In reality, Coolidge was known to take daily two-hour naps.

A lively breakfast with artists went against Silent Cal's typecasting, and just like with the Easter Parade emancipators, it led to front page news across the country. Coolidge won 54 percent of the vote in a three-way race in the 1924 election. Bernays explained his role in the Library of Congress collection, *Prosperity and Thrift: The Coolidge Era and the Consumer Economy, 1921–1929*: "I was applying an old press agent technique of adding newsworthy names to the austere person of the President of the United States in an event that jutted out of the routine of circumstance and made news."

Edward Bernays has been dead for over a quarter of a century. He was born before radio, television and movies and died at the birth of the internet and the world wide web. He's noted for his elite corporate clients, but also handled national publicity in 1920 for the NAACP's eleventh annual conference in Atlanta, Georgia, the first held outside a northern city. Bernays laid out a case for curbing the Great Northward Migration by associating the political economy prospects of African Americans with Southern economic interests. Other causes were not so progressive. He was the chief propagandist for the United Fruit Company (later known as Chiquita Brands

International) that back then controlled 42 percent of the land in Guatemala. He advised the country to support a CIA-backed military coup in 1954 with its "army of liberation" to overthrow the democratically-elected Arbenz administration that had bought back company land for use by 100,000 poor families. This time the newspaper headlines were not so friendly, condemning the coup as a form of "economic colonialism."

Harold Burson, CEO and co-founder of one of the world's largest public relations firm, Burson-Marsteller, once said, "We're still singing off the hymn book that Bernays gave us." This endorsement came from a man who was named by *PR Week* "the most influential P.R. person of the 20th century," but whose firm also represented nation rebranding trade and tourism campaigns for dictatorial regimes in Argentina, Romania, and Nigeria. In his 1965 autobiography, Bernays revealed his shock that Joseph Goebbels, Hitler's Reichsminister of Public Enlightenment and Propaganda, had used *Crystallizing Public Opinion* for guidance in a deliberate and planned campaign of destruction against the Jewish people. We all are left to ponder what Bernays would advise for overt acts in support of client interests in an ocean of trolling farms and character assassination Twitter wars. Where would improper-ganda end and proper-ganda begin? This book will provide some clues.

—**NANCY SNOW**, May 2021

The
Edward Bernays
Reader

Manipulating Public Opinion:
The Why and The How
(1928)

PUBLIC OPINION IS SUBJECT TO A variety of influences that develop and alter its views on nearly every phase of life today. Religion, science, art, commerce, industry are in a state of motion. The inertia of society and institutions is constantly combated by the activity of individuals with strong convictions and desires.

Civilization, however, is limited by inertia. We repeat constantly our beliefs and habits until they become a cumulative retrogressive force. Our attitude toward social intercourse, toward economics, toward national and international politics continues past attitudes and strengthens them under the force of tradition. Comstock lets his mantle of proselytizing morality fall on a willing Sumner; Penrose lets fall his mantle on Butler; Carnegie his on Schwab; and ad infinitum. Opposing this traditional acceptance of existing ideas is an active public opinion that has been directed consciously into movement against inertia. Public opinion was made or changed formerly by tribal chiefs, by kings, by religious leaders. Today the privilege of attempting to sway public opinion is everyone's. It is one of the manifestations of democracy that anyone may try to convince others and to assume leadership on behalf of his own thesis.

Narrowly defined, public opinion represents the thought of any given group of society at any given time toward a given object. Looked at from the broadest standpoint, it is the power of the group to sway the larger public in its attitude toward ideas.

New ideas, new precedents, are continually striving for a place in the scheme of things. Very often these ideas are socially sound and constructive and put an end to worn-out notions. Usually they are minority ideas, for naturally, but regrettably, majority ideas are most often old ones. Public opinion is slow and reactionary, and does not easily accept new ideas.

The innovator, the leader, the special pleader for new ideas, has through necessity developed a new technique—the psychology of public persuasion. Through the application of this new psychology he is able to bring about changes in public opinion that will make for the acceptance of new doctrines, beliefs, and habits. The manipulation of the public mind, which is so marked a characteristic of society today, serves a social purpose. This manipulation serves to gain acceptance for new ideas. It is a species of education in that it presents new problems for study and consideration to the public, and leaves it free to approve or reject them. Never before was so broad a section of the general public so subjected to facts on both sides of so many problems of life. Honest education and honest propaganda have much in common. There is this dissimilarity: Education attempts to be disinterested, while propaganda is frankly partisan.

What are the various motives for the manipulation of public opinion? They are the motives which dominate man in our society today. The basic instincts of self-preservation, procreation, and love are the more complex social motives. People attempt to sway other people for social motives—ethical, philanthropic, educational—for political, for international, for economic, and for motives of personal ambition.

From a social motive a special pleader may wage a campaign against tuberculosis or cancer, or to raise the standard of business ethics, or to secure support for a philanthropic institution. From the political standpoint, he may strive to make the public accept the idea of specific efficiency or economy in government. Internationally a special pleader may be seeking peace among the nations. Or in economics he may try to create a new market for an old product, or a market for a new product. Personal ambition to succeed, to convince others, to win recognition are basic motives that have activated most of the leaders of the world.

There is, of course, one danger inherent in this essential machinery of dealing with public opinion. It is a danger so grave that editors and publicists shy from the subject rather than discuss it.

Where shall we end, they say, in this welter of conflicting ideas? What will come from this chaos? And cannot the man who has manipulated his public opinion and won it to his side misuse it for his own purpose? Possibly he can. There are Ku Klux Klans, there are Mussolinis, there are tyrannies of every sort; but a public that learns more and more how to express itself will learn more and more how to overthrow tyranny of every sort. So that every man who teaches the public how to ask for what it wants is at the same time teaching the public how to safeguard itself against his own possible tyrannous aggressiveness.

How is public opinion manipulated? The technique of measuring and recording human relations has not been perfected as has the technique of measuring physical relations. No Bureau of Standards with micrometers exists for the expert on human or public relations. Experimental psychology has provided some yardsticks, but they are not clearly defined and are more easily applied to one field of manipulated public opinion—advertising—than to the broader field of propaganda or public relations.

It is comparatively simple to test out the comparative efficacy of a page advertisement with white space and an advertisement which is printed solidly, or on a colored billboard and a black-and-white billboard. But the method of the experimental psychological laboratories hardly meets the requirements of the technician who deals with public opinion in the broad.

Here the specialist in swaying public opinion avails himself of the findings of introspective psychology. He knows in general the basic emotions and desires of the public he intends to reach, and their prevalence and intensity. Analysis is the first step in dealing with a problem that concerns the public. He employs the technique of statistics, field-surveying, and the various methods of eliciting facts and opinions in examining both the public, and the idea or product he seeks to propagandize.

Diagnostic ability enters into this question of manipulating public opinion; a diagnostic ability that is perhaps a greater essential in manipulating public opinion effectively today than it will be later, when the technique has been more scientifically developed.

Sociology also contributes to his technique. The group cleavages of society, the importance of group leaders, and the habits of their followers are part of the technical background of his work. He has methods adapted to educating the public to new ideas, to articulating minority ideas and strengthening them, to making latent majority ideas active, to making an old principle apply to a new idea, to substituting ideas by changing cliches, to overcoming prejudices, to making a part stand for the whole, and to creating events and circumstances that stand for his ideas. He must know the physical organs of approach to his public: the radio, the lecture platform, the motion picture, the letter, the advertisement, the pamphlet, the newspaper. He must know how an idea can be translated into terms that fit any given form of communication, and that his public can understand.

An interesting experiment is being conducted in New York in an endeavor to chart these human relationships along scientific lines. The first study of this group was to trace the development and functioning of given attitudes toward given subjects, such as religion, sex, race, morality, nationalism, internationalism, and so forth. The conclusion was established that attitudes were often created by a circumstance or circumstances of dramatic moment. Very often the propagandist is called upon to create a circumstance that will eventuate in the desired reaction on the part of the public he is endeavoring to reach.

So much for principle; how, in practice, does this manipulating process work out?

Take the question of the fight against lynching, Jim Crowism, and the civil discriminations against the Negro below the Mason and Dixon line. How was public opinion manipulated after the war to bring about a change, or at least a modification for the better, in the public attitude toward the Negro? The National Association for the Advancement of Colored People had the fight in hand. As a matter of technique, they decided to dramatize the year's campaign in an annual convention which would center attention at one time and at one place upon the ideas they stood for and upon the men who stood for these ideas. The purpose of this convention was to build up for the question and for its proponents the support of all those who would necessarily learn of the conference.

The first step in the technique settled, the next step was to decide how to make it most effective.

Should it be held in the North, South, West, or East? Since the purpose was to affect the entire country, the Association was advised to hold it in the South. For, said the propagandist, a point of view on a southern question, emanating from a southern center, would have a greater force of authority than the same point of view issuing from any other locality, particularly when that point of view was at odds with the traditional southern point of view. Atlanta was chosen.

The third step was to surround the conference with people who were stereotypes for ideas that carried weight all over the country. The support of leaders of diversified groups was sought. Telegrams and letters were dispatched to leaders of religious, political, social, and educational groups, asking for their point of view on the purpose of the conference. But in addition to these group leaders of national standing it was particularly important from the technical standpoint to secure the opinions of group leaders of the South, even from Atlanta itself, to emphasize the purposes of the conference to the entire public. There was one group in Atlanta which could be approached. A group of ministers, on the basis of Christianity, had been bold enough to come out for a greater interracial amity. This group was approached and agreed to co-operate in the conference.

Here, then, were the main factors of a created circumstance; a conference to be held in a southern city, with the participation of national leaders and especially with the participation of southern gentlemen. The scene had been set. The acts of the play followed logically.

And the event ran off as scheduled. The program itself followed the general scheme. Negroes and white men from the South on the same platform, expressing the same point of view.

A dramatic element spotlighted here and there. A national leader from Massachusetts, descendant of an Abolitionist, agreeing in principle and in practice with a Baptist preacher from the South.

If the radio had been in effect, the whole country would have heard and been moved by the speeches and the principles expressed.

But the public read the words and the ideas in the press of the country. For the event had been created of such important component parts as to awaken interest throughout the country and to gain support for its ideas even in the South.

The editorials in the southern press, reflecting the public opinion of their communities, showed that the subject had become one of interest to the editors because of the participation by southern leaders.

The event naturally gave the Association itself substantial weapons with which to appeal to an increasingly wider circle. Further expansion of these thoughts was attained by mailing reports, letters, and other documents to selected groups of the public. Who can tell what homes, what smoking-rooms in Pullman cars and hotels, what schoolrooms, what churches, what Rotary and Kiwanis clubs responded to the keynote struck by these men and women speaking in Atlanta.

As for the practical results, the immediate one was a change in the minds of many southern editors who realized that the question at issue was not an emotional one, but a discussable one; and that this point of view was immediately reflected to their readers. As for the further results, these are hard to measure with a slide rule. The conference had its effect in changing the attitude of southerners; it had its definite effect in building up the racial consciousness and solidarity of the Negroes; it had its effect in bringing to the South in a very dramatic way a realization of the problems it was facing, with the consequent desire among its leaders to face them more ably. It is evident that the decline in lynching is an effect of this and other efforts of the Association.

But let us touch another field, that of industry. The millinery industry two years ago was hanging by a thread. The felt hat had arrived and was crowding out the manufacture of all those kinds of hats and hat ornaments upon which an industry and thousands of men and women employed in it had subsisted. What to do to prevent debacle?

A public relations counsel was called in by the association of the millinery trade, both wholesale and retail. He analyzed the hat situation and found that the hats made by the manufacturer could roughly be classified into six groups: the lace hat, the ribbon hat, the straw and feather-trimmed and other ornamented hats, and so on.

The public relations counsel tabulated the elements of the social structure that dominated the hat-using habits of women. These he found comprised four classes: First, the society leader, the woman at the fountainhead of style who made the fashion by her approval. Second, there was the style expert, the writer or publicist who enunciated fashion facts and information. Third was the artist, who was needed to give artistic approval to the styles. Fourth, and not unimportant either, were beautiful women to wear the embodied ideas sanctioned by the other groups. The problem, then, was to bring into juxtaposition all of these groups, and preferably at one time and at one place, before an audience of those most concerned, the buyers of hats.

With that as a working plan of how to shape events to bring about the desired result, the remainder of the work was simply filling in the outline with real people.

A committee of prominent artists was organized to choose the six most beautiful girls in New York to wear, in a series of six tableaux, the six most beautiful hats of the six style classifications at a fashion fete to be held at the Hotel Astor. Heyworth Campbell, art editor of the Conde Nast publications, was head of the committee. Leo Lentelli, the sculptor; Charles Dana Gibson; Henry Creange, the art director; Ray Greenleaf, joined the group and toiled mightily to choose from among hundreds of applicants the six most desirable candidates.

In the meantime there was organized a style committee of distinguished American women who, on a basis of their interest in the development of an American industry, were willing to add the authority of their names to the idea. And, simultaneously, there was organized a style committee consisting of Carmel White, of *Vogue*, and other prominent fashion authorities who were willing to support the idea because of its style value. The girls had been chosen.

Now they chose the hats.

On the evening of the fashion show everything had been

arranged for the dramatic juxtaposition of all of these elements for molding public opinion. The girls—beautiful girls—in their lovely hats and costumes paraded on the running-board before an audience of the entire trade.

The news of the event affected not only the buying habits of the onlookers, but also of the women throughout the country. The story of the event was flashed to the consumer by the news service of her newspaper as well as by the advertisement of her favorite store. Broadsides went to the millinery buyer from the manufacturer, and the rotogravure of the lovely women in the lovely hats went to the consumer in the smallest town. In ten days the industry was humming. One manufacturer stated that whereas before the show he had not sold any large-trimmed hats, after it he sold thousands. The felt hat was put to rout; not by Paris immediately, but by the women in this country, who quite rightly accepted the leadership of the fashion groups who had created the circumstances as they are outlined here.

If large-trimmed hats could put to rout the small felt cloche, then perhaps velvet could also make its inroads upon the style habits of twenty-three million women. Analysis showed that the velvet manufacturers could not start their fashion here. Fashion came from Paris. That Lyons, home of silk manufactories, and Paris, home of couturieres and milliners, influenced the American markets, both of manufacture and distribution, there was no doubt. The attack had to be made at the source. It was determined to substitute purpose for chance, and to utilize the regular sources for fashion distribution, and to influence the public from the sources. A velvet fashion service, openly supported by the manufacturers, was organized. Its first function was to establish contact with the Lyons manufactories and the Paris couturieres to find out what they were doing, to encourage them to act on behalf of velvet, and to help in the proper exploitation of their wares. An intelligent Parisian was enlisted into the work. It was he who visited Lanvin and Worth, Agnes and Patou, etc., and induced them to use velvet in their gowns and their hats. It was he who arranged for the distinguished Countess this or Duchess that to wear the hat or the gown. And as for the presentation of the idea to the public, the American buyer or the American woman of fashion was simply shown the velvet creations in the atelier of the dressmaker or the milliner. She bought the velvet because she liked it and because it was in fashion. The editor of the American magazine and the fashion reporter of the American newspaper, likewise subjected to the actual (though created) circumstance, reflected it in her news, which, in turn, subjected the consumer and the buyer here to the same influences. The result was that what was at first a trickle of velvet became a flood. A demand was slowly being created, not fortuitously, but consciously. A big department store, aiming to be a style leader, advertised velvet gowns and hats on the authority of French couturieres and quoted original cables received from them. The echo of the new style note resounded from hundreds of department stores throughout the country who wanted to be style leaders too.

Broadside followed broadside, the mail followed the cables, and the American woman traveler appeared before ship news photographers in velvet gown and hat.

The created circumstances had their effect. Velvet was the fashion. "Fickle fashion had veered to velvet," was one newspaper comment. And the industry in South Manchester and Patterson again kept thousands busy.

•

The fields in which public opinion can be manipulated to conform to a desired result are as varied as life itself.

In politics, for instance, in order to humanize an individual: When President Coolidge was running for office the question was brought up of how the hitherto unknown personality of the man in the White House could be projected to the country.

It was suggested that an event in which the most human groups would be brought into juxtaposition with the president would have the desired result. Actors and actresses were invited to breakfast with Mr. Coolidge at the White House. The country felt that a man in the White House who could laugh with Al Jolson and the Dolly sisters was not frigid and unsympathetic.

An interesting example of international propaganda is the campaign that was waged to make 110,000,000 people in America realize that a small country on the Baltic was not simply a spot on the map. Lithuania was reflected to this country in its drama, music, literature, habits, economics, and agriculture. The printed word and events created to symbolize facts and ideas made America aware of the conditions in Lithuania and of its just aspirations. Ignorance was dissipated and sympathies strengthened to a point where these feelings became translated into action. Lithuania received economic aid and political recognition.

From Lithuania to silks is a long distance. And yet the same technique of creating circumstance which freed the Lithuanians helped to create a market for more beautiful silks. Although the silks made in America were inspired by France, the American woman refused to recognize their style of beauty until Paris had put its stamp of approval on them. That was the problem: to develop public opinion to accept the idea that American silk was artistic, and to use French authority in accomplishing that end. The silks were authentic in beauty, workmanship, and style. A plan was developed to have the silks exhibited in the Louvre, because that stands for the idea of accredited beauty in the American mind. It was suggested that the American ambassador officially open the exhibition, as a fitting recognition of America's leadership in the field. He felt legitimately that he was doing his duty in encouraging American industry. Leading men and women in the French capital were invited to the exhibition, with the consequence that by cable, by motion picture, by mail, the American public was soon made conscious of the fact that its own silk had received the recognition of the French art authorities. It must be good, therefore! And the best index of the success of the plan was the fact that the leading cities of the United States vied with each other for the honor of exhibiting what the Louvre had shown, whereas before they had regarded the productions of America's looms simply as so much merchandise.

As for the companies interested in gaining acceptance for new inventions, how can they overcome the inertia of the public without applying some stimulus to public opinion? The panatrope, an instrument which is the result of years of painstaking experimentation in the electrical and acoustical laboratories of four great corporations—the Westinghouse, the General Electric, the Radio Corporation, and the Brunswick-Balke-Collender companies—was perfected and ready for general sale. A definite technique must be used to launch it to affect the minds of millions who presumably are much more interested in football scores and Lindbergh than in a new mechanical principle in music-making machinery. Group adherence is the fulcrum around which broad acceptance for new ideas can most rapidly be moved. Certain small groups are important enough to influence the attitudes of large groups that overlap them. First were the music lovers and critics, whose acceptance of this new idea carried weight with the average buyer of musical instruments, who without their aid could not formulate an opinion as to the quality of this machine. Scientists were selected to join the committee of sponsorship that had been formed. Their support of the idea meant to the public that it was scientifically correct. Third was the stereotype of the Metropolitan Opera House, which stands in the public mind for achievement in music. It was decided to gather all of these elements together at a single dramatic event in a place which should further symbolize the idea. The patrons of music were chosen: Mrs. Vincent Astor and Mr. Otto Kahn joined the committee. The scientists, John Hays Hammond and Doctor Alfred N. Goldsmith, were happy to give their authority to the idea and joined the committee. Benjamino Gigli, a tenor of the Metropolitan Opera Company, gave the artistic stamp of approval to the event. And quite naturally Aeolian Hall, the nucleus of music, was chosen as the place at which the event was to be held. A representative audience responded to the invitation. The event was important and interesting and took a prominent place among the competitive ideas and events of the day. The consequence was that the Panatrope immediately received acceptance as an important musical instrument. Without the definite procedure of implanting a new idea in the public mind, the inertia of society might have retarded the acceptance of this invention in the musical field for many years.

Public opinion may be marshaled for or against even salad dressings. Here the American's sense of humor was made the basis of a plan to make large numbers of the public receptive to a new product. Reciprocal relations between the palate and the palette in terms of harmonies in oil were made the basis of a picturesque joke. The public, more seriously occupied with Chinese revolutions and Nicaraguan questions, responded immediately to the idea that art galleries are fitting places, not only for still-lifes of salads as painted by famous artists, but also of examples of art in cooking. Beautifully prepared salads dedicated to famous artists were therefore displayed underneath canvases painted by famous artists. The exhibit was colorful and spirited and had its effect in focusing attention on salad dressing. That newspapers offer space in their columns and devote time and attention to such an exhibit is not the relevant point. What is relevant is that an idea may strike the fancy and arrest the attention of hundreds of thousands of people, and as such can be communicated to them through every form of thought-transmission of which modern business avails itself.

Analysis of the problem and its causes is the first step toward shaping the public mind on any subject. Occasionally the analysis points to a basic change in the policy of a manufacturer.

Take the case of a certain vegetable shortening. There was no sale of this food product in certain sections of the public. A careful research was made. It was found that Orthodox Jews would not buy it because it did not conform to the dietary requirements of their religion. The manufacturer altered the product itself to make it conform to the dietary strictures of this market. The problem that lay before him then was to acquaint this sector of the population with the change. This problem was handled with success. The stamp of approval was given the product by religious leaders and special dietary officials. Institutions such as hospitals, that were known to conform scrupulously to the dietary rules, were asked to convince themselves of the character and quality of the product. Their approval bore weight with the thousands of people who respected their authority.

One method of changing people's ideas has been often used, and that is to substitute new ideas for old by changing *cliches*. The evacuation hospitals during the war came in for a certain amount of criticism because of the summary way in which they handled their wounded. The name was changed to "evacuation post," thus changing the cliche. No one expected more than adequate emergency treatment of an institution so named. This story, which was told to me by a reliable authority, is a clear illustration of the principle.

Before 1925 few people in America felt that industry had any connection with art. Few manufacturers thought seriously of the artistic ramifications of their work. A small group of people, however, realizing the importance of this phase of American industry, approached Herbert Hoover, Secretary of Commerce, and suggested that he appoint a commission to visit and report on the International Exposition of Industrial and Decorative Arts at Paris in 1925. I was appointed associate commissioner. We appointed about 150 delegates from different industries to study the exposition at Paris. A report was made. Industry itself became conscious of the new cliche of themselves that had been made in this way. Since then a determined progress toward authentic beauty has been made in large industries throughout the country.

Soap found a new market and a new use when the public

relations counsel of a large soap corporation called upon the desire for beauty of a strong minority of the population and introduced soap as a medium for sculpture as a pastime for children and as an educational aid for schools. An annual contest has been held for several years in a leading art gallery, and exhibits of the works of thousands of professional and amateur sculptors shown in the leading galleries and museums of the country.

Instantaneous attention was given to the financial articles of W. Z. Ripley, asking for full publicity in financial reports of stock corporations. He articulated an idea that was latent in the minds of a large majority of the public. The next step was to convert this new awareness into action. Public opinion, aroused by Ripley, forced the New York Stock Exchange to take action.

Occasionally the manipulation of the public mind entails the removal of a prejudice. Prejudices are often the application of old taboos to new conditions. They are illogical, emotional, and hampering to progress. Take, for example, the feeling that used to exist against margarine. In its early stages of manufacture in this country, margarine was, like as not, made of impure animal matter. Its state of wholesomeness was not apparent. Today margarine is made of pure vegetable or animal ingredients that have been scientifically determined upon as wholesome and passed as pure by the government. Yet the prejudice carried over, and a difficult campaign is still being waged to remove this prejudice. Correspondence is carried on with officials and leaders in the field of medicine, hygiene, and dietetics, and the result of their manifold study given out to the public. The prejudice remained long after its cause had been altered.

This is an age of mass production. In the mass production of materials a broad technique has been developed and applied to their distribution. In this age, too, there must be a technique for the mass distribution of ideas. Public opinion can be moved, directed, and formed by such a technique. But at the core of this great heterogeneous body of public opinion is a tenacious will to live, to progress, to move in the direction of ultimate social and individual benefit. He who seeks to manipulate public opinion must always heed it.

The Engineering of Consent
(1947)

FREEDOM OF SPEECH AND ITS DEMOCRATIC corollary, a free press, have tacitly expanded our Bill of Rights to include the right of persuasion. This development was an inevitable result of the expansion of the media of free speech and persuasion. All these media provide open doors to the public mind. Any one of us through these media may influence the attitudes and actions of our fellow citizens.

The tremendous expansion of communications in the United States has given this Nation the world's most penetrating and effective apparatus for the transmission of ideas. Every resident is constantly exposed to the impact of our vast network of communications which reach every corner of the country, no matter how remote or isolated. Words hammer continually at the eyes and ears of America. The United States has become a small room in which a single whisper is magnified thousands of times.

Knowledge of how to use this enormous amplifying system becomes a matter of primary concern to those who are interested in socially constructive action.

There are two main divisions of this communications system which maintain social cohesion. On the first level there are the commercial media. Almost 1,800 daily newspapers in the United States have a combined circulation of around 44,000,000. There are approximately 10,000 weekly newspapers and almost 6,000 magazines. Approximately 2,000 radio stations of various types broadcast to the nation's 60,000,000 receiving sets. Approximately 16,500 motion picture houses have a capacity of almost 10,500,000. A deluge of books and pamphlets is published annually. The country is blanketed with billboards, handbills, throwaways, and direct mail advertising. Round tables, panels and forums, classrooms and legislative assemblies, and public platforms—any and all media, day after day, spread the word, someone's word.

On the second level there are the specialized media owned and operated by the many organized groups in this country. Almost all such groups (and many of their subdivisions) have their own communications systems. They disseminate ideas not only by means of the formal written word in labor papers, house organs, special bulletins, and the like, but also through lectures, meetings, discussions, and rank-and-file conversations.

LEADERSHIP THROUGH COMMUNICATION

This web of communications, sometimes duplicating, crisscrossing, and overlapping, is a condition of fact, not theory. We must recognize the significance of modern communications not only as a highly organized mechanical web but as a potent force for social good or possible evil. We can determine whether this network shall be employed to its greatest extent for sound social ends.

For only by mastering the techniques of communication can leadership be exercised fruitfully in the vast complex that is modern democracy in the United States. In an earlier age, in a society that was small geographically and with a more homogeneous population, a leader was usually known to his followers personally; there was a visual relationship between them. Communication was accomplished principally by personal announcement to an audience or through a relatively primitive printing press. Books, pamphlets, and newspapers reached a very small literate segment of the public.

We are tired of hearing repeated the threadbare cliché "The world has grown smaller"; but this so-called truism is not actually true, by any means. The world has grown both smaller and very much larger. Its physical frontiers have been expanded. Today's leaders have become more remote physically from the public; yet, at the same time, the public has much greater familiarity with these leaders through the system of modern communications. Leaders are just as potent today as ever.

In turn, by use of this system, which has constantly expanded as a result of technological improvement, leaders have been able to overcome the problems of geographical distance and social stratification to reach their publics. Underlying much of this expansion, and largely the reason for its existence in its present form, has been the widespread and enormously rapid diffusion of literacy.

Leaders may be the spokesmen for many different points of view. They may direct the activities of major organized groups such as industry, labor, or units of government. They may compete with one another in battles for public good will; or they may, representing divisions within the larger units, compete among themselves. Such leaders, with the aid of technicians in the field who have specialized in utilizing the channels of communication, have been able to accomplish purposefully and scientifically what we have termed "the engineering of consent."

THE ENGINEERING APPROACH

This phrase quite simply means the use of an engineering approach— that is, action based only on thorough knowledge of the situation and on the application of scientific principles and tried practices to the task of getting people to support ideas and programs. Any person or organization depends ultimately on public approval, and is therefore faced with the problem of engineering the public's *consent* to a program or goal. We expect our elected government officials to try to engineer our consent—through the network of communications open to them—for the measures they propose. We reject government authoritarianism or regimentation, but we are willing to take action suggested to us by the written or spoken word. The engineering of consent is the very essence of the democratic process, the freedom to persuade and suggest. The freedoms of speech, press, petition, and assembly, the freedoms which make the engineering of consent possible, are among the most cherished guarantees of the Constitution of the United States.

The engineering of consent should be based theoretically and practically on the complete understanding of those whom it attempts to win over. But it is sometimes impossible to reach joint decisions based on an understanding of facts by all the people. The average American adult has only six years of schooling behind him. With pressing crises and decisions to be faced, a leader frequently cannot wait for the people to arrive at even general understanding. In certain cases, democratic leaders must play their part in leading the public through the engineering of consent to socially constructive goals and values. This role naturally imposes upon them the obligation to use the educational processes, as well as other available techniques, to bring about as complete an understanding as possible.

Under no circumstances should the engineering of consent supersede or displace the functions of the educational system, either formal or informal, in bringing about understanding by the people as a basis for their action. The engineering of consent often does supplement the educational process. If higher general educational standards were to prevail in this country and the general level of public knowledge and understanding were raised as a result, this approach would still retain its value.

Even in a society of a perfectionist educational standard, equal progress would not be achieved in every field. There would always be time lags, blind spots, and points of weakness; and the engineering of consent would still be essential. The engineering of consent will always be needed as an adjunct to, or a partner of, the educational process.

IMPORTANCE OF ENGINEERING CONSENT

Today it is impossible to overestimate the importance of engineering consent; it affects almost every aspect of our daily lives. When used for social purposes, it is among our most valuable contributions to the efficient functioning of modern society. The techniques can be subverted; demagogues can utilize the techniques for antidemocratic purposes with as much success as can those who employ them for socially desirable ends. The responsible leader, to accomplish social objectives, must therefore be constantly aware of the possibilities of subversion. He must apply his energies to mastering the operational know-how of consent engineering, and to out-maneuvering his opponents in the public interest.

It is clear that a leader in a democracy need not always possess the personal qualities of a Daniel Webster or a Henry Clay. He need not be visible or even audible to his audiences. He may lead indirectly, simply by effectively using today's means of making contact with the eyes and ears of those audiences. Even the direct, or what might be called the old-fashioned, method of speaking to an audience is for the most part once removed; for usually public speech is transmitted, mechanically, through the mass media of radio, motion pictures, and television.

During World War I, the famous Committee on Public Information, organized by George Creel, dramatized in the public's consciousness the effectiveness of the war of words. The Committee helped to build the morale of our own people, to win over the neutrals, and to disrupt the enemy. It helped to win that war. But by comparison with the enormous scope of word warfare in World War II, the Committee on Public Information used primitive tools to do an important job. The Office of War Information alone probably broadcast more words over its short-wave facilities during the war than were written by all of George Creel's staff.

As this approach came to be recognized as the key factor in influencing public thought, thousands of experts in many related fields came to the fore—such specialists as editors, publishers, advertising men, heads of pressure groups and political parties, educators, and publicists. During World War I and the immediate postwar years a new profession developed in response to the demand for trained, skilled specialists to advise others on the technique of engineering public consent, a profession providing counsel on public relations.

THE PROFESSIONAL VIEWPOINT

In 1923 I defined this profession in my book, *Crystallizing Public Opinion,* and in the same year, at New York University, gave the first course on the subject. In the almost quarter-century that has elapsed since then, the profession has become a recognized one in this country and has spread to other democratic countries where free communication and competition of ideas in the marketplace are permitted. The profession has its literature, its training courses, an increasing number of practitioners, and a growing recognition of social responsibility.

In the United States, the profession deals specifically with the problems of relationship between a group and its public. Its chief function is to analyze objectively and realistically the position of its client vis-a-vis a public and to advise as to the necessary corrections in its client's attitudes toward and approaches to that public. It is thus an instrument for achieving adjustment if any maladjustment in relationships exists. It must be remembered of course that good will, the basis of lasting adjustment, can be preserved in the long run only by those whose actions warrant it. But this does not prevent those who do not deserve good will from winning it and holding onto it long enough to do a lot of damage.

The public relations counsel has a professional responsibility to push only those ideas he can respect, and not to promote causes or accept assignments for clients he considers antisocial.

PLANNING A CAMPAIGN

Just as the civil engineer must analyze every element of the situation before he builds a bridge, so the engineer of consent, in order to achieve a worthwhile social objective, must operate from a foundation of soundly planned action. Let us assume that he is engaged in a specific task. His plans must be based on four prerequisites:

1. Calculation of resources, both human and physical; i.e., the manpower, the money, and the time available for the purpose;

2. As thorough knowledge of the subject as possible;

3. Determination of objectives, subject to possible change after research; specifically, what is to be accomplished, with whom and through whom;

4. Research of the public to learn why and how it acts, both individually and as a group.

Only after this preliminary groundwork has been firmly laid is it possible to know whether the objectives are realistically attainable. Only then can the engineer of consent utilize his resources of manpower, money, and time, and the media available. Strategy, organization, and activities will be geared to the realities of the situation.

The task must first be related to the budget available for manpower and mechanics. In terms of human assets, the consent engineer has certain talents—creative, administrative, executive—and he must know what these are. He should also have a clear knowledge of his limitations. The human assets need to be implemented by work space and office equipment. All material needs must be provided by budget.

Above all else, once the budget has been established, and before a first step is taken, the field of knowledge dealing with the subject should be thoroughly explored. This is primarily a matter of collecting and codifying a store of information so that it will be available for practical, efficient use. This preliminary work may be tedious and exacting, but it cannot be by-passed; for the engineer of consent should be powerfully equipped with facts, with truths, with evidence, before he begins to show himself before a public.

The consent engineer should provide himself with the standard reference books on public relations, publicity, public opinion: N. W. Ayer & Son's *Directory of Newspapers and Periodicals*, the *Editor and Publisher Year Book*, the *Radio Daily Annual*, the *Congressional Directory*, the *Chicago Daily News Almanac*, the *World Almanac*—and, of course, the telephone book. (The *World Almanac*, for example, contains lists of many of the thousands of associations in the United States—a cross section of the country.) These and other volumes provide a basic library necessary to effective planning.

At this point in the preparatory work, the engineer of consent should consider the objectives of his activity. He should have clearly in mind at all times precisely where he is going and what he wishes to accomplish. He may intensify already existing favorable attitudes; he may induce those holding favorable attitudes to take constructive action; he may convert disbelievers; he may disrupt certain antagonistic points of view.

Goals should be defined exactly. In a Red Cross drive, for example, a time limit and the amount of money to be raised are set from the start. Much better results are obtained in a relief drive when the appeal is made for aid to the people of a specific country or locality rather than of a general area such as Europe or Asia.

STUDYING THE PUBLIC

The objective must at all times be related to the public whose consent is to be obtained. That public is people, but what do they know? What are their present attitudes toward the situation with which the consent engineer is concerned? What are the impulses which govern these attitudes? What ideas are the people ready to absorb? What are they ready to do, given an effective stimulant? Do they get their ideas from bartenders, letter carriers, waitresses, Little Orphan Annie, or the editorial page of the *New York Times*? What group leaders or opinion molders effectively influence the thought process of what followers? What is the flow of ideas—from whom to whom? To what extent do authority, factual evidence, precision, reason, tradition, and emotion play a part in the acceptance of these ideas?

The public's attitudes, assumptions, ideas, or prejudices result from definite influences. One must try to find out what they are in any situation in which one is working.

If the engineer of consent is to plan effectively, he must also know the group formations with which he is to deal, for democratic society is actually only a loose aggregate of constituent groups. Certain individuals with common social and/or professional interests form voluntary groups. These include such great professional organizations as those of doctors, lawyers, nurses, and the like; the trade associations; the farm associations and labor unions; the women's clubs; the religious groups; and the thousands of clubs and fraternal associations. Formal groups, such as political units, may range from organized minorities to the large amorphous political bodies that are our two major parties. There is today even another category of the public group which must be kept in mind by the engineer of consent. The readers of the *New Republic* or the listeners to Raymond Swing's program are as much voluntary groups, although unorganized, as are the members of a trade union or a Rotary Club.

To function well, almost all organized groups elect or select leaders who usually remain in a controlling position for stated intervals of time. These leaders reflect their followers' wishes and work to promote their interests. In a democratic society, they can only lead them as far as, and in the direction in which, they want to go. To influence the public, the engineer of consent works with and through group leaders and opinion molders on every level.

VALUE AND TECHNIQUES OF RESEARCH

To achieve accurate working knowledge of the receptivity of the public mind to an idea or ideas, it is necessary to engage in painstaking research. Such research should aim to establish a common denominator between the researcher and the public. It should disclose the realities of the objective situation in which the engineer of consent has to work. Completed, it provides a blueprint of action and clarifies the question of who does what, where, when, and why. It will indicate the overall strategy to be employed, the themes to be stressed, the organization needed, the use of media, and the day-to-day tactics. It should further indicate how long it will take to win the public and what are the short- and long-term trends of public thinking. It will disclose subconscious and conscious motivations in public thought, and the actions, words, and pictures that effect these motivations. It will reveal public awareness, the low or high visibility of ideas in the public mind.

Research may indicate the necessity to modify original objectives, to enlarge or contract the planned goal, or to change actions and methods. In short, it furnishes the equivalent of the mariner's chart, the architect's blueprint, the traveler's road map. Public opinion research may be conducted by questionnaires, by personal interviews, or by polls. Contact can be made with business leaders, heads of trade associations, trade union officials, and educational leaders, all of whom may be willing to aid the engineer of consent. The heads of professional groups in the communities— the medical association, the architects, the engineers—all should be queried. So should social service executives, officials of women's clubs, and religious leaders. Editors, publishers, and radio station and motion picture people can be persuaded to discuss with the consent engineer his objectives and the appeals and angles that affect these leaders and their audiences. The local unions or associations of barbers, railwaymen, clothing workers, and taxicab drivers may be willing to co-operate in the undertaking. Grass-roots leaders are important. Such a survey has a double-barreled effect. The engineer of consent learns what group leaders know and do not know, the extent to which they will cooperate with him, the media that reach them, appeals that may be valid, and the prejudices, the legends, or the facts by which they live. He is able simultaneously to determine whether or not they will conduct informational campaigns in their own right, and thus supplement his activities.

THEMES, STRATEGY, AND ORGANIZATION

Now that the preliminary work has been done, it will be possible to proceed to actual planning. From the survey of opinion will emerge the major themes of strategy. These themes contain the ideas to be conveyed; they channel the lines of approach to the public; and they must be expressed through whatever media are used. The themes are ever present but intangible—comparable to what in fiction is called the "story line." To be successful, the themes must appeal to the motives of the public. Motives are the activation of both conscious and subconscious pressures created by the force of desires. Psychologists have isolated a number of compelling appeals, the validity of which has been repeatedly proved in practical application. Once the themes are established, in what kind of a campaign are they to be used? The situation may call for a blitzkrieg or a continuing battle, a combination of both, or some other strategy. It may be necessary to develop a plan of action for an election that will be over in a few weeks or months, or for a campaign that may take years, such as the effort to cut down the tuberculosis death rate.

Planning for mass persuasion is governed by many factors that call upon all one's powers of training, experience, skill, and judgment. Planning should be flexible and provide for changed conditions. When the plans have been perfected, organization of resources follows, and it must be undertaken in advance to provide the necessary manpower, money, and physical equipment. Organization also correlates the activities of any specialists who may be called upon from time to time, such as opinion researchers, fund raisers, publicity men, radio and motion picture experts, specialists for women's clubs and foreign language groups, and the like.

THE TACTICS

At this point it will be possible to plan the tactics of the program, i.e., to decide how the themes are to be disseminated over the idea carriers, the networks of communication.

Do not think of tactics in terms of segmental approaches. The problem is not to get articles into a newspaper or obtain radio time or arrange a motion picture newsreel; it is rather to set in motion a broad activity, the success of which depends on interlocking all phases and elements of the proposed strategy, implemented by tactics that are timed to the moment of maximum effectiveness. An action held over but one day may fall completely flat. Skilled and imaginative timing has determined the success of many mass movements and campaigns, the familiar phenomena so typical of the American people's behavior pattern. Emphasis of the consent engineer's activities will be on the written and spoken word, geared to the media and designed for the audiences he is addressing. He must be sure that his material fits his public. He must prepare copy written in simple language and sixteen-word sentences for the average school-age public. Some copy will be aimed at the understanding of people who have had seventeen years of schooling. He must familiarize himself with all media and know how to supply them with material suitable in quantity and quality.

Primarily, however, the engineer of consent must create news. News is not an inanimate thing. It is the overt act that makes news, and news in turn shapes the attitudes and actions of people. A good criterion as to whether something is or is not news is whether the event juts out of the pattern of routine. The developing of events and circumstances that are not routine is one of the basic functions of the engineer of consent. Events so planned can be projected over the communication systems to infinitely more people than those actually participating, and such events vividly dramatize ideas for those who do not witness the events. The imaginatively managed event can compete successfully with other events for attention. Newsworthy events, involving people, usually do not happen by accident. They are planned deliberately to accomplish a purpose, to influence our ideas and actions.

Events may also be set up in chain reaction. By harnessing the energies of group leaders, the engineer of consent can stimulate them to set in motion activities of their own. They will organize additional, specialized, subsidiary events, all of which will further dramatize the basic theme.

CONCLUSION

Communication is the key to engineering consent for social action. But it is not enough to get out leaflets and bulletins on the mimeograph machines, to place releases in the newspapers, or to fill the air waves with radio talks. Words, sounds, and pictures accomplish little unless they are the tools of a soundly thought-out plan and carefully organized methods. If the plans are well formulated and the proper use is made of them, the ideas conveyed by the words will become part and parcel of the people themselves. When the public is convinced of the soundness of an idea, it will proceed to action. People translate an idea into action suggested by the idea itself, whether it is ideological, political, or social. They may adopt a philosophy that stresses racial and religious tolerance; they may vote a New Deal into office; or they may organize a consumers' buying strike. But such results do not just happen. In a democracy they can be accomplished principally by the engineering of consent.

Molding Public Opinion
(1935)

A PUBLIC OPINION HAS SUDDENLY EMERGED as an entity that must be considered and intelligently dealt with in any endeavor involving the public or any part of it. World War propaganda showed the possibilities of molding public opinion towards an objective. Its success convinced leaders how vital it is to gauge public reaction to ideas or products; how necessary it is to get public support for any project of consequence.

As civilization has grown more complex, the transmission of ideas has been quickened. As competitive forces have multiplied and sharpened, it has become increasingly apparent to all groups that they must win and obtain public approval if they are to survive in the welter of competing forces struggling for public favor.

This recognition has led to the development of a new type of technician—the counsel on public relations—on whose advice many individuals and groups rely. The function of the public relations counsel is to interpret his client to the public, and the public to his client. In its logical extension, it is to bring about a harmony of understanding between nation and nation, government and the people, charitable institutions and contributors, private corporation and its public, or between any group and the public which that group serves and upon whose good will it is dependent.

The propagandist can be a force for constructive or destructive ends. This is not unique with his profession. It is a condition which prevails in other professions and businesses as well. Certainly forces for the public good should use the weapon. Let us consider for a moment some of the high spots in the background of public opinion, the field in which the counsel on public relations works.

THE PUBLIC

Who is the public? The words, "molding public opinion," assume the existence of a united, cohesive public. Such a public can exist perhaps in times of a vital need or emergency. But ordinarily, what we call the public is made up of a great many smaller publics or groups banded together because of some common interest.

A political tactician, in planning his campaign, first roughly classifies his public into those who are for him and do not need to be propagandized, those who are against him, and those who may be swayed but do not belong definitely to either of the two other groups. Such an analysis of the public is simple and elementary. But it is only rarely that the public can be so definitely classified.

Sometimes the public may be classified according to geographical distribution. Or it may be divided according to age groups. Mussolini and Hitler, for example, place great emphasis on youth movements, and utilize the influence of the young to sway the more temperate adult groups. In some cases, the public is divided according to sex, financial classifications, occupational classifications, economic or political beliefs, or social groups in the narrower sense. There may be classification according to reading habits, intellectual capacities, positions as leaders or followers, positions as employers or employed, religious affiliations, racial and national derivations, or special interests in sports, philanthropies, hobbies, or clubs.

GROUP LEADERSHIP

Here, then, is a first element in molding public opinion. How can the propagandist reach these groups who make up the large public? He can reach them through their leaders, for the individual looks for leadership to the leaders of the groups to which he belongs. He may be dominated by the leaders of many groups, for these group cleavages of society are numerous and diversified. They play a vital part in molding public opinion, and they offer the propagandist a means of reaching vast numbers of individuals; for with so many confusing and conflicting ideas competing for the individual's attention, he is forced to look to others for authority and leadership. No man, in today's complicated world, can base his judgments and acts entirely on his own examination and weighing of the evidence. A credence in leaders is a sound short-cut (when leaders are sound).

Thus the group leader becomes a key figure in the molding of public opinion, and his acceptance of a given idea carries with it the acceptance of many of his followers—through many channels. If group leaders accept our ideas, the groups they dominate will respond. The importance of these key leaders as a medium for reaching large groups of the population is a factor of primary importance, and must never be neglected. Nor must we forget that not only do they convey ideas to the public, but they also interpret and articulate to the propagandist, for his guidance, the particular groups they represent. In their entirety, they represent the whole public.

Pressure groups today are at the basis of movements that gain wide acceptance. We may define a "pressure group" as any group of people interested enough in an idea to support it actively. Active participation in such a group may take no more tangible form than writing a letter or attending a meeting. Nearly all Americans fall into some such group, many into several; and it is through group cohesion and group leadership that one can awaken public interest most speedily and constructively. The success of prohibition repeal was achieved, not by directly converting millions of people, but by enlisting the active support of leaders of groups to which millions of people belonged.

HUMAN MOTIVATIONS

Behind all these divisions and affiliations of individual members of the public, a second factor must be borne in mind by the propagandist. What are the great basic motivations of people, wherever they are and to whatever groups they belong? Self-preservation, ambition, pride, hunger, love of family and children, patriotism, imitativeness, the desire to be a leader, love of play—these and others are the psychological raw materials of which every leader must be aware in his endeavor to win the public to his point of view.

The propagandist must analyze his problem in its relationship to the underlying motives of the people and the groups to which they belong. He must therefore resolve his case into terms that will appeal to fundamental motives in such a way as to get the attention and support of the leaders of the vast system of interlocking groups making up his public, as well as of their publics. The milk industry, for instance, recognizing that milk has marked qualities that appeal to the self-preservation motive of human beings, finds that health, nutrition, and other authorities will of *their own* accord emphasize these qualities of milk to their public.

SYMBOLS

A public relations campaign must take into consideration the group relationships of society and the dominant instincts of people. It must also reckon with the validity of symbols, which is the third point in this discussion of the background of public relations. A symbol may be defined as a short-cut to understanding and to action. It is the currency of propaganda. Often it is a word. The connection established by the "wets" between the words "racketeer" and "prohibition" undoubtedly influenced public opinion against prohibition. The acceptance of the symbol is emotional and an expression of familiarity. That symbols must be carefully chosen is self-evident. In publicizing a vast corporation, the symbol may be a single person at the head of the organization; it may be a slogan describing the product; or it may be a single department which performs a specific public service.

It is the function of the public relations program to associate the special pleading with ideas to which the public is receptive. The potency of symbols is constantly changing. They must be utilized intelligently at every opportunity. Commentators on propaganda technique have occasionally stated that this is a method that attempts to gain adherents for a point of view by an appeal to the emotions instead of to the brain. This is, of course, a re-defining of the word as propagandists know it. The propagandist uses every sound method available to him to project his ideas.

THE MEDIA

We come to the fourth factor which the propagandist must keep in mind at all times—the media by which his facts and his point of view reach his public.

In the vast system which has grown up today for the production and dissemination of ideas, there are many media through which ideas come to the public minute by minute and day by day. Cameras, microphones, printing presses, and typewriters are multitudinously busy presenting, through these media, the opinions of A to B, C, and D; presenting facts collected by E to F, G, and H; and reporting events created by I for the benefit of J, K, and L.

Let us list a few of these media which I have catalogued under the printed word—including advertising, of course. The figures given are obviously approximate.

Daily newspapers (U. S.)…	2,000
Weekly newspapers (U. S.)…	6,300
Semi-weekly newspapers (U. S.)…	350
Circulation of daily newspapers (U.S. and Canada)…	38,700,000
Sunday circulation…	26,700,000
Religious publications…	690
Class and trade publications…	2,500
Miscellaneous publications of all types…	3,800
New books published (1933)…	6,813
Billboards…	200,000

Direct-by-mail, telegrams, cables, and the like also fall under the classification of the printed word.

Under the spoken word we have, with their approximate numbers:

Radio stations (U. S.) ...	600
Radio sets ...	18,500,000
Churches ...	232,000
Legitimate theaters ...	
Chautauquas reaching thousands of people ...	
Telephones (U. S) ...	16,800,000[*]
Women's Clubs ...	14,500
Rotary Clubs, Lions Clubs, service clubs, businessmen's clubs, and the like ...	

Under the graphic or pictorial classification, we have, with their approximate numbers :

Motion picture houses (U. S.) ...	22,000
Seating capacity ...	11,300,000
Picture showings in public schools in one year ...	44,000
Rotogravure sections in 63 newspapers with a circulation of millions ...	
Numerous services providing pictures for the small daily ...	
Display of news pictures all over the United States, as window displays, and the like	
Traveling exhibits, exhibits in museums, libraries, and the like.	

---

[*] "which may be interconnected," Dec. 31, 1934. Cf. American Telephone and Telegraph Co., *Report*, 1934, pp. 1, 18.

We have called attention to these figures in order to make the point that this organization of communication in the United States enables practically any person or any group or any movement to be brought almost immediately into the closest juxtaposition with people almost anywhere. This is one important fact which makes the control or the modification of mass behavior possible in the United States. The control over mass behavior is obviously tremendously augmented if ideas are effectively projected through these media. The individual cannot ignore effective appeals through these channels, especially when the appeals are based on dominant motives and have the support of group leaders.

Every one is a propagandist for some platform, and it is the freedom with which all may employ the methods of propaganda that makes for safety and stability in a democratic country. No man or group of men in this country has ever had a monopolistic control of methods or media. There are no patents by which one can control the dissemination of opinion. There is no coercion by which any man can prevent any group of free adult people in America from opposing ideas disseminated by others. The great safeguard to propaganda methods in this country is that there is always freedom of counter-propaganda available here. In that regard we differ from Fascist and Communist regimes. The freedom of counter-propaganda must go hand in hand with the freedom of speech, of the press, and of the right to peaceable assembly—fundamentals of democracy.

FOUR STEPS ESSENTIAL TO FORMULATE A PROGRAM

Let us turn now to the more specific steps that have to be taken in formulating a public relations program. For the sake of making this outline more specific let us assume that the program is for an industry. Four steps are indicated:

1. *Formulation of objectives*

The first point is the formulation of just what the objectives are. This is the basic step. Under our competitive system, the private profit motive and the public interest must coincide. If the objectives are not in the public interest, the program should be abandoned.

2. *Analysis of public attitude*

The second point is the analysis of the attitude of the public towards the industry and the services it renders.

Obviously, such an analysis must be based on a broad and representative survey which should answer such questions as: What is the general attitude of the public towards the products and service provided? How do specific actions and broad policies of the industry affect the public's attitude? In what ways does the industry fail to measure up to what the public expects of it?

Such a study should also reveal any fundamental changes that are taking place in public opinion, so that the industry may either make whatever changes may be indicated to conform to new public demands, or endeavor to educate the public to its own point of view wherever public demands seem impossible of fulfillment.

This survey will provide a scientific foundation on which the industry can base its public relations program and, if necessary, make indicated changes in the conduct of its business. Such studies bring to light numerous important facts that could not be obtained through the usual relationships between salesmen and customers. Such a survey, too, should give the industry a better perspective of all the other products and services that are competing with what it has to sell.

3. *Study of analysis*

Taking up the third step, a study of this analysis should then be made with a view to keynoting the approach to the public in terms of action of the industry. This action must be continuous over a period of time. It must be overt wherever possible. It must be conceived in terms of the public's interest, in so far as this coincides with the industry's own private interest.

Such a public relations program or policy must be integrated into the entire functioning of the industry. It cannot be something that is simply superimposed on the organization. It cannot be lip worship to an idea. It cannot consist merely of releases from a mimeograph machine. It must be part and parcel of the thinking and action of the leaders in the industry. And it may mean that such thinking and action must be decidedly changed in order to conform to public demand and public objectives. Ideas that are not generally accepted by the public can be made acceptable only if they can be shown to be of value to the public, and if their appeal can be related to acceptable facts, opinions, or customs. Symbols must be valid as well as vital.

In commerce and industry, only recently has the idea of enlightened self-interest become effective. Corporations are appreciating that the self-interest of the corporation can best be served if it promotes the public interest. Life insurance companies have realized that their interest in the public health has been of financial benefit to the companies. A radio instrument manufacturing company in trying to sell good radios realizes the value of stimulating a more constructive and discriminating interest in radio broadcast programs themselves.

The policy to be established must reconcile the actual objective with the preconceptions, the preoccupations, and the existing attitudes of the many sections of the public. The policy determined on may be simply a policy of the most profound and widespread fact-finding, and subsequent presentation of the facts to an individual, a group, or the general public. The policy may require the formulation of a program to educate the public on the broad issues involved, or it may require an active offensive on behalf of a particular fact.

The determination of a basic policy is of supreme importance in any propagandist move. Merely to express opinion, no matter how well, may be of little value or definitely harmful to the cause, if it does not specifically meet the underlying needs of the situation.

4. *Use of media*

After such a program has been laid out on paper and decided upon in terms of broad policy, the fourth step—the actual carrying out of such a policy—can begin. This is the projection and interpretation of the industry through all possible media, in terms of what the public is thinking and demanding.

The first principle of such a campaign is that it must have continuity. Isolated approaches are of little value. The effort must be carefully planned so that the effect of the effort may become cumulatively powerful. The structure of the campaign must be as progressive and unified as the erection of a building.

We have already enumerated many of the media to be considered. The old-time press agent sent pieces to the paper; the propagandist today may wage an entire campaign without sending a single release to the newspapers. The media are still important, and they may be utilized to the utmost, but they must be utilized with discrimination. Certain ideas are more effective when transmitted through certain media. A thousand people marching may be more convincing than a thousand words, or vice versa, depending upon the circumstances.

Not only must these media be selected with care, but the objective—in whatever form expressed—must be stated in terms of the particular medium desired. This means that the objective will have to be dramatized so that the basic ideas it represents stand out in the welter of competing ideas and flow naturally to the public through the accustomed channels.

Events will have to be developed which will symbolize the objectives and at the same time be interesting enough to be utilized in the various channels that reach the public. Support must be obtained from leaders of the public, and this support reflected to the public. Symbols must be selected. Once a searching study of public attitudes has been made, and the program coordinated with these attitudes, many channels that reach the public will be found.

This paper has attempted to give a dispassionate outline of the techniques and the media involved in the molding of public opinion by any group. No attempt has been made to discuss the social significance of this new development in our complex civilization. Obviously, every group interested in social advancement must base its approach to its problems on a recognition of the principles and practices as brought out in this outline of the subject.

Attitude Polls—
Servants or Masters?
(1945)

LIKE VITAMINS AND SO MANY OTHER good things, attitude polls have been adopted by America with its customary unthinking enthusiasm for new things. Polls are an enormously useful implement when honestly, efficiently and intelligently gathered and understood. On the other hand, they are potentially dangerous weapons in the hands of the unwise, the inept, the dishonest or the anti-social.

Not all polls are honestly conducted, not all polls are accurately taken, not all polls are intelligently interpreted, polls rarely educe future attitudes. Nevertheless, the public scans the figures with devotion and believes that the verdict of the majority has been given for all time on all the questions answered in these polls.

Public and leaders tend to regard attitude polls today as the voice of God and the will of the people. They have a new magic for satisfying the ancient desire to learn tomorrow's lesson from yesterday's page.

Many different kinds of attitude polls claim to photograph the public's point of view on every form of enterprise, private and public, profit and nonprofit. Some ask simple yes and no attitudes. Others are broader and check answers through multiple questions. Some polls, scientific and accurate, cross-section the public before questioning starts. Such polls are "quota sampling," "area sampling," and "panel polls." Some bring out superficial attitudes. Others go deeper. Some are made once; others are spread at intervals over a period.

The discussion in this article covers only attitude polls. It does not apply to factual and purely quantitative surveys on markets, elections and other similar measurement studies. Nor does it apply to depth interviews which are not really polls although some people regard them as such. Depth surveys can indicate future trends. They try to discover the motives of people, try to find out why they think and act as they do. They find out what attitudes are permanent, what words, pictures, actions fix them, which attitudes can be changed, and how.

Polls are a highly useful technique when properly used as a guide to current opinion. Notable work is being done in America today in these attitude measurements. We agree with Pendleton Herring of Harvard who recently said in the *American Political Science Review*: "The leadership in public opinion research is today in the capable hands of Hadley Cantril, Elmo Roper, George Gallup, Samuel Stouffer, Rensis Likert and their numerous fellow workers. The work of these men and their skill in polling opinion is of direct utility to officials and policy makers. Moreover, their invention of new tools of analysis and their creation of new sources for data are a boon to workers in various fields."

But too many leaders and too much of the public accept attitude polls with simple faith. They should not do so. The value of polls lies in interpretation as well as in their accuracy. An attitude poll, in itself, conveys no message. Figures of a poll are the raw material. A poll is an index to the future only if the interpreter knows a good deal more than the figures of the poll show in themselves. Millions of Americans do not know that the poll is a flash of light that reveals only a split second attitude.

Polls deserve serious consideration by government, pollster and the public. We need to define the function of polls; to call attention to the dangers to society of misinterpretation, misuse and distortion; to show why polls vary as indices of future action of people.

Inaccurate polls and interpretations are a danger to society:–

1. Because inaccurate polls have as strong an influence on the public as true polls.

2. Because misuse of polls, for biased or venal purposes by pollsters or by those who hire pollsters, can be extremely harmful.

3. Because leaders who misinterpret and distort polls in dealing with the public are a menace to society.

THE BASIC DANGER

There is too literal an acceptance of the validity of attitude polls. Many people believe that when a poll shows 51 per cent of the public favoring a proposition, that this is the will of the public. This belief by leader and public tends to eliminate traditionally democratic ways of making decisions by accommodation and adjustment of the viewpoints of majority and minority groups. The decisions were usually fought out in the open through discussion and compromise. Today the poll has muffled dissenting voices. That is a real danger to our democratic way of arriving at conclusions.

Even inaccurate and inept attitude polls influence the public.

One recent case illustrates this point dramatically. The effect of an inaccurate election poll on the fortunes of a defeated political party was summed up by its chairman in a telegram to Governor Dewey. The poll was taken by the *New York Daily News*. The telegram was sent by the Liberal Party: "On Oct. 15 the *News* poll erroneously predicted a vote of over 70 per cent for Mr. O'Dwyer. (The actual vote was 57.3 percent.) From that day on the campaign for good government was over for all practical purposes. Morale sagged, workers disappeared and revenues stopped."

But such a danger exists not only in the case of the inaccurate polls. It is equally strong in the case of accurate polls. In the recent Jeffries-Frankensteen election, the undue influence of polls was dramatically brought before the public. The Opinion Research Corporation had been hired by a private party under contract to make an attitude poll of the chances of election of the two candidates. The *Detroit Free Press* got hold of the poll and published it. It showed an overwhelming percentage of the Negroes in Detroit were in favor of Frankensteen. Frankensteen charged that the poll adversely affected his election because of this showing.

There are dangers from the use of stacked, false, phony polls for biased or venal purposes. Polls are a temptation to pollsters or to groups which, without social responsibility, use polls for their own ends knowing the credence the public gives them.

POLLS VS. LEADERS

Attitude polls often lull legislators and business men into the belief that they are safe from public disapproval when quantitative percentage corroborates their own point of view. They do not think of public opinion as subject to change without notice, and disregard such possibility. They do not consider the passive or hidden points of view as important. This may lead to explosions later on when minority opinions become articulate, active and overt and come suddenly into open conflict with majority opinion. Discussions are important in making decisions in the broad public interest.

There is, too, the danger in the new kind of leadership which polls have produced in the United States—leadership of obedience to polls. Correct polls must be carefully used:

1. Because attitude polls exercise so strong an influence upon the public as often to discourage use of sound democratic methods of reaching important decisions.
2. Because society suffers when polls inhibit leaders from independent thinking, from anticipating change or from preparing the public for change.
3. Because polls exert pressure that may place society under what Jefferson called the tyranny of the majority and throttle progressive minority ideas.

We are no longer led by men. We are led around by the polls. The obligation of democratic leadership, whether in business or politics, is to inform and educate public opinion towards worthwhile progress, and make decisions on a more careful basis than making merely a numerical count. Attitude polls have become deciding factors in politics, the arts, business and, in fact, every phase of our life.

This leaves the public unprepared for change because leaders who should, do not prepare the public for change. We know that attitudes are changed very quickly by planned action, by unplanned events, even though developmental change is usually slow. The people who pin their faith on the permanency of attitudes as shown by polls, and therefore believe they are accurate forecasts, are often misled. Social, industrial and political leaders who follow the polls, follow the past instead of advancing to the future. Society suffers.

Because their true value is distorted in the public mind, polls may also destroy progressive action of many kinds by intimidating leaders. They prevent the over-cautious from proceeding forward along progressive lines. People examine the figures and obey them. If there is a 70 per cent poll vote in favor of a product, a traffic regulation, a proposed Congressional bill, the poll makes up the leaders' minds. Their reason for bowing to the poll is very simple. Why should they stick their necks out by going against what seems to be majority opinion?

This is not to say that the leader follows his public. By and large, real leaders in our national life are almost invariably ahead of their followers. But pseudo-leaders, who in most cases actually are followers, are encouraged by the polls to be followers.

The present belief that polls show a permanent public opinion helps to maintain the status quo. Certainly in a fast moving world this is a dead weight. Majorities must be stimulated and educated to move ahead. The danger to society from destroying initiative is self evident.

But while the attitude polls carry these dangers with them, scientifically planned polls, carried out within the limits of present-day knowledge, may be accurate as to future actions. They can forecast elections. Five of them, for instance, forecast the outcome of the last presidential race with errors of less than 2 per cent from the actual popular vote. Possibly one reason scientific attitude polls are so correct in election forecasts is that voting in this country is carried on largely along traditional lines. According to social psychologists, the election is usually decided long before the campaigning starts. Only a small percentage of the vote is flexible.

LIKE AN ICEBERG...

It is a far cry from the validity of polls of this kind to polls collecting public attitudes towards billboard advertising, radio commercials or child labor. For such polls to have meaning, figures must be studied and interpreted in the light of a broader analysis of public trends, counter drives and significant events.

The voice of the people which pollsters say is expressed in attitude polls, is rarely the unchangeable voice of the people. Public opinion is like an iceberg. The visible portion is the expressed attitudes, but the submerged portion of public opinion is sometimes potentially the more powerful.

The scientific poll is a count of the public's current feelings. While it tells public reaction only at the moment when the count is taken, it can be useful. It can serve as a tool of leadership. The polls may aid in making plans, in attempting to strengthen public attitudes or to change them. Socially-minded leaders try to know public attitudes at a given moment. With this knowledge, they can plan to educate the public on the value of new customs, new attitudes, or they can help to preserve present ones.

When I talk of leadership, I mean democratic leadership— leadership through democratic methods, through education, through persuasion, not leadership by threat, intimidation, force or hypocrisy as practiced in authoritarian regimes. In politics, democratic progress is reached through the interaction of individuals and groups led by individuals towards a common decision. A leader in America can proceed no faster than his followers want to follow him. The true function of attitude polls then is to be a tool to aid leaders to fulfill their democratic function in business or politics. For the public, the poll should be simply a thermometer—it shows the temperature at the moment of taking practiced in authoritarian regimes. In politics, democratic progress is reached through the interaction of individuals and groups led by individuals towards a common decision.

Most attitudes are subject to change through outside pressure. Here, as Dr. Hadley Cantril (of Princeton University's Office of Public Opinion Research) says, we must distinguish between "polls that touch deep-seated, well-crystallized attitudes and those that touch uncrystallized situations—it's the latter that polls, leaders or any other influence can affect."

To interpret a poll from figures alone is like diagnosing a patient by only reading the thermometer. Even readings over a period are ineffective in polls. The figures may remain stable over a period and may lead to a wrong interpretation, namely, forecasting by projecting stable attitudes into the future. Actually, the public may be apathetic or ignorant of a condition. Tomorrow they may learn new facts which may change their attitude.

Public attitudes as shown by polls, although correct at any given moment, may vary upwards or downwards when words, pictures and actions are used to change these attitudes. Or these attitudes may be maintained when words, pictures and actions intensify present attitudes.

When the United States destroyer, the *Panay*, was sunk by the Japanese before the war, negative attitudes toward Japan in the United States moved up sharply overnight. Publicity given to one botulinus death from an olive changed attitudes swiftly from favorable to unfavorable. When Sonja Henie wore white leather skating shoes in a motion picture, thousands of girls rushed to buy white skating shoes instead of traditional black shoes.

Authority or factual evidence dramatically presented may modify attitudes. So may effective reasoning or persuasion appealing to tradition or emotion. Pollsters recognize this. But, nevertheless, too many people regard attitude polls as if they showed unchangeable attitudes.

THE WHY

What are some of the reasons why attitude polls vary as indices of future action of the people; why do they not fill the functions that leaders and people think they do; and why do they need to be interpreted judgmatically? The psychological factors I am going to discuss are of course obvious. The reason I talk of them is because they indicate how one can get a mass opinion that is not really valid, but nevertheless can exert a powerful influence.

Attitude polls may represent only what an individual may want to tell an inquirer or what he thinks the inquirer wants to hear. Often they represent merely a man's conforming to the generally accepted point of view. Unconscious censorship often prevents the interviewee from saying what he really thinks—or may do. A man who says on Monday he isn't prejudiced against Negroes, may join a lynching party on Tuesday. Sometimes answers are bandwagon answers. Sometimes the answer is an attempt to build up his ego or to impress the hearer with the respondent's status. Answers may reflect environmental or other external conditions of the moment.

The way a question is asked, the technique of the individual pollster, affect the validity of an attitude poll. The pollster's bias and point of view have an influence. The personality of the questioner affects the man who is interviewed. The answer depends on the psychosomatic condition of the inquirer as well as the respondent. Emotions of the moment have a great effect on answers given on the spur of the moment. They slant a quick answer and may lead to direct misstatements. A man who has had a hearty breakfast, a good night's sleep and looks forward to a pleasant day will answer differently than he would have if he had been out all night, had had a little too much to drink, or is disturbed about a family situation. A man on his way to the doctor may be more pessimistic about taxes than the same man who has just been told by the doctor that his blood pressure is okay. No one felt too good about anything the day after the Nazi invasion of Paris. Such widespread moods don't cancel one another out, so that the law of averages does not always apply.

Our unconscious thought as well as our conscious reasonings affect answers. What we answer is sometimes a rationalization. The real reasons may be hidden because we are ashamed of them. They may be frivolous or selfish reasons of which we disapprove.

Many people are neurotic. Their answers may reflect their inner struggle with themselves and may not show their real point of view. For any number of reasons—glandular, psychological, social—we may avoid a considered answer on the spur of the moment. All these factors would play a part in the meaning any attitude poll would have.

Some attitude polls give only a quantitative measurement based on yes and no answers. These do not show whether a man will change his point of view or not, or why, because they do not show intensity of attitude. The intensity with which an attitude is held indicates the potential of change. That is why so many polls are poor guides to anything but the thought of the moment. That is why the attitudes presented by polls may change tomorrow or the next day.

TWO RECOMMENDATIONS

What can be done to prevent some of the misuse, the distortions and misinterpretations of polls? Here are two recommendations. I believe they deserve discussion and action.

1. The people, as represented by their state or national government, must insure themselves against malpractice of any profession fraught with the public interest. This is done in the case of doctors, lawyers, accountants and architects by setting up standards of character and educational qualifications before an individual is permitted to practice.

Licenses should be required for the practice of polling. Every sound practitioner undoubtedly would welcome such a step. Self-regulation has been practiced by many professions, and can be set up in the polling profession.

The suggestion has been made that this might be done by a nongovernmental body taking over supervision of pollsters. This is possible, but it is doubtful whether a private organization would have the authority in the public mind that government would, to eliminate phony, stacked, venal, dishonest and inaccurate polls.

There is one other step—the protection of the public and its leaders.

2. Educational activities, aimed at public and leaders, must be carried on to acquaint them with the significance of polls in our society. They should be given facts and points of view about polls, so that they can appraise polls correctly and in that way prevent dangers to society. Releases about polls should discuss weighting, if there has been any, should give the facts and figures of regional or sectional divisions in order to give a better understanding of the many constituent groups that enter into majority action.

Polls then will fill a sound democratic purpose of helping make decisions represent the accommodation of many viewpoints, rather than a majority opinion overwhelming all other points of view.

From *Propaganda* (1928)

CHAPTER II:
THE NEW PROPAGANDA

IN THE DAYS WHEN KINGS WERE kings, Louis XIV made his modest remark, "L'Etat c'est moi." He was nearly right.

But times have changed. The steam engine, the multiple press, and the public school, that trio of the industrial revolution, have taken the power away from kings and given it to the people. The people actually gained power which the king lost. For economic power tends to draw after it political power; and the history of the industrial revolution shows how that power passed from the king and the aristocracy to the bourgeoisie. Universal suffrage and universal schooling reinforced this tendency, and at last even the bourgeoisie stood in fear of the common people. For the masses promised to become king.

Today, however, a reaction has set in. The minority has discovered a powerful help in influencing majorities. It has been found possible to so mold the mind of the masses that they will throw their newly gained strength in the desired direction. In the present structure of society, this practice is inevitable. Whatever of social importance is done today, whether in politics, finance, manufacture, agriculture, charity, education, or other fields, must be done with the help of propaganda. Propaganda is the executive arm of the invisible government.

Universal literacy was supposed to educate the common man to control his environment. Once he could read and write he would have a mind fit to rule. So ran the democratic doctrine. But instead of a mind, universal literacy has given him rubber stamps, rubber stamps inked with advertising slogans, with editorials, with published scientific data, with the trivialities of the tabloids and the platitudes of history, but quite innocent of original thought. Each man's rubber stamps are the duplicates of millions of others, so that when those millions are exposed to the same stimuli, all received identical imprints. It may seem an exaggeration to say that the American public gets most of its ideas in this wholesale fashion. The mechanism by which ideas are disseminated on a large scale is propaganda, in the broad sense of an organized effort to spread a particular belief or doctrine.

I am aware that the word propaganda carries to many minds an unpleasant connotation. Yet whether, in any instance, propaganda is good or bad depends upon the merit of the cause urged, and the correctness of the information published.

In itself, the word propaganda has certain technical meanings which, like most things in this world, are "neither good nor bad but custom makes them so." I find the word defined in Funk and Wagnall's Dictionary in four ways: "

1. A society of cardinals, the overseers of foreign missions; also the College of Propaganda at Rome founded by Pope Urban VIII in 1627 for education of missionary priests; Sacred College de Propaganda Fide.

2. "Hence, any institution or scheme for propagating a

doctrine or system.

3. Effort directed systematically toward the gaining of public support for an opinion or a course of action.

4. "The principles advanced by a propaganda."

The *Scientific American*, in a recent issue, pleads for the restoration to respectable usage of that "fine old word 'propaganda.'"

"There is no word in the English language," it says, "whose meaning has been so sadly distorted as the word 'propaganda.' The change took place mainly during the late war when the term took on a decidedly sinister complexion."

"If you turn to the *Standard Dictionary*, you will find that the word was applied to a congregation or society of cardinals for the care and oversight of foreign missions which was instituted at Rome in the year 1627. It was applied also to the College of the Propaganda at Rome that was founded by Pope Urban VIII, for the education of the missionary priests. Hence, in later years the word came to be applied to any institution or scheme for propagating a doctrine or system."

"Judged by this definition, we can see that in its true sense propaganda is a perfectly legitimate form of human activity. Any society, whether it be social, religious or political, which is possessed of certain beliefs, and sets out to make them known, either by the spoken or written words, is practicing propaganda."

"Truth is mighty and must prevail, and if any body of men believe that they have discovered a valuable truth, it is not merely their privilege but their duty to disseminate that truth. If they realize, as they quickly must, that this spreading of the truth can be done upon a large scale and effectively only by organized effort, they will make use of the press and the platform as the best means to give it wide circulation. Propaganda becomes vicious and reprehensive only when its authors consciously and deliberately disseminate what they know to be lies, or when they aim at effects which they know to be prejudicial to the common good."

"'Propaganda' in its proper meaning is a perfectly wholesome word, of honest parentage, and with an honorable history. The fact that it should today be carrying a sinister meaning merely shows how much of the child remains in the average adult. A group of citizens writes and talks in favor of a certain course of action in some debatable question, believing that it is promoting the best interest of the community. Propaganda? Not a bit of it. Just a plain forceful statement of truth. But let another group of citizens express opposing views, and they are promptly labeled with the sinister name of propaganda . . ."

"'What is sauce for the goose is sauce for gander,' says a wise old proverb. Let us make haste to put this fine old word back where it belongs, and restore its dignified significance for the use of our children and our children's children."

The extent to which propaganda shapes the progress of affairs about us may surprise even well informed persons. Nevertheless, it is only necessary to look under the surface of the newspaper for a hint as to propaganda's authority over public opinion. Page one of the *New York Times* on the day these paragraphs are written contains eight important news stories. Four of them, or one-half, are propaganda. The casual reader accepts them as accounts of spontaneous happenings. But are they? Here are the headlines which announce them:

"TWELVE NATIONS WARN CHINA REAL REFORM
MUST COME BEFORE THEY GIVE RELIEF,"
"PRITCHETT REPORTS ZIONISM WILL FAIL,"
"REALTY MEN DEMAND A TRANSIT INQUIRY,"
"OUR LIVING STANDARD HIGHEST IN HISTORY,
SAYS HOOVER REPORT,"

Take them in order: The article on China explains the joint report of the Commission on Extraterritoriality in China, presenting an exposition of the Powers' stand in the Chinese muddle. What it says is less important than what it is. It was "made public by the State Department today" with the purpose of presenting to the American public a picture of the State Department's position. Its source gives it authority, and the American public tends to accept and support the State Department view.

The report of Dr. Pritchett, a trustee of the Carnegie Foundation for International Peace, is an attempt to find the facts about this Jewish colony in the midst of a restless Arab world. When Dr. Pritchett's survey convinced him that in the long run Zionism would "bring more bitterness and more unhappiness both for the Jew and for the Arab," this point of view was broadcast with all the authority of the Carnegie Foundation, so that the public would hear and believe. The statement by the president of the Real Estate Board of New York, and Secretary Hoover's report, are similar attempts to influence the public toward an opinion.

These examples are not given to create the impression that there is anything sinister about propaganda. They are set down rather to illustrate how conscious direction is given to events, and how the men behind these events influence public opinion. As such they are examples of modern propaganda. At this point we may attempt to define propaganda.

Modern propaganda is a consistent, enduring effort to create or shape events to influence the relations of the public to an enterprise, idea or group.

This practice of creating circumstances and of creating pictures in the minds of millions of persons is very common. Virtually no important undertaking is now carried on without it, whether the enterprise be building a cathedral, endowing a university, marketing a moving picture, floating a large bond issue, or electing a president. Sometimes the effect on the public is created by a professional propagandist, sometimes by an amateur deputed for the job. The important thing is that it is universal and continuous; and in its sum total it is regimenting the public mind every bit as much as an army regiments the bodies of its soldiers.

So vast are the numbers of minds which can be regimented, and so tenacious are they when regimented, that a group at times offers an irresistible pressure before which legislators, editors, and teachers are helpless. The group will cling to its stereotypes, as Walter Lippmann calls it, making of those supposedly powerful beings, the leaders of public opinion, mere bits of driftwood in the surf. When an Imperial Wizard, sensing what is perhaps hunger for an ideal, offers a picture of a nation all Nordic and nationalistic, the common man of the older American stock, feeling himself elbowed out of his rightful position and prosperity by the newer immigrant stocks, grasps the picture which fits in so neatly with his prejudices, and makes it his own. He buys the sheet and pillowcase costume, and bands with his fellows by the thousand into a huge group powerful enough to swing state elections and to throw a ponderous monkey wrench into a national convention.

In our present social organization approval of the public is essential to any large undertaking. Hence a laudable movement may be lost unless it impresses itself on the public mind. Charity, as well as business, and politics and literature, for that matter, have had to adopt propaganda, for the public must be regimented into giving money just as it must be regimented into tuberculosis prophylaxis. The Near East Relief, the Association for the Improvement of the Condition of the Poor of New York, and all the rest, have to work on public opinion just as though they had tubes of toothpaste to sell. We are proud of our diminishing infant death rate—and that too is the work of propaganda.

Propaganda does exist on all sides of us, and it does change our mental pictures of the world. Even if this be unduly pessimistic—and that remains to be proved—the opinion reflects a tendency that is undoubtedly real. In fact, its use is growing as its efficiency in gaining public support is recognized.

This then evidently indicates the fact that anyone with sufficient influence can lead sections of the public, at least for a time and for a given purpose. Formerly the rulers were the leaders. They laid out the course of history, by the simple process of doing what they wanted. And if nowadays the successors of the rulers, those whose position or ability gives them power, can no longer do what they want without the approval of the masses, they find in propaganda a tool which is increasingly powerful in gaining that approval. Therefore, propaganda is here to stay.

It was, of course, the astounding success of propaganda during the war that opened the eyes of the intelligent few in all departments of life to the possibilities of regimenting the public mind. The American government and numerous patriotic agencies developed a technique which, to most persons accustomed to bidding for public acceptance, was new. They not only appealed to the individual by means of every approach—visual, graphic, and auditory—to support the national endeavor, but they also secured the cooperation of the key men in every group—persons whose mere word carried authority to hundreds or thousands or hundreds of thousands of followers. They thus automatically gained the support of fraternal, religious, commercial, patriotic, social, and local groups whose members took their opinions from their accustomed leaders and spokesmen, or from the periodical publications which they were accustomed to read and believe. At the same time, the manipulators of patriotic opinion made use of the mental clichés and the emotional habits of the public to produce mass reactions against the alleged atrocities, the terror, and the tyranny of the enemy. It was only natural, after the war ended, that intelligent persons should ask themselves whether it was possible to apply a similar technique to the problems of peace.

As a matter of fact, the practice of propaganda since the war has assumed very different forms from those prevalent twenty years ago. This new technique may fairly be called the new propaganda.

It takes account not merely of the individual, nor even of the mass mind alone, but also and especially of the anatomy of society, with its interlocking group formations and loyalties. It sees the individual not only as a cell in the social organism but as a cell organized into the social unit. Touch a nerve at a sensitive spot and you get an automatic response from certain specific members of the organism.

Business offers graphic examples of the effect that may be produced upon the public by interested groups, such as textile manufacturers losing their markets. This problem arose, not long ago, when the velvet manufacturers were facing ruin because their product had long been out of fashion. Analysis showed that it was impossible to revive a velvet fashion within America. Anatomical hunt for the vital spot! Paris! Obviously! But yes and no. Paris is the home of fashion. Lyons is the home of silk. The attack had to be made at the source. It was determined to substitute purpose for chance and to utilize the regular sources for fashion distribution and to influence the public from these sources. A velvet fashion service, openly supported by the manufacturers, was organized. Its first function was to establish contact with the Lyons manufactories and the Paris couturiers to discover what they were doing, to encourage them to act on behalf of velvet, and to help in the proper exploitation of their wares. An intelligent Parisian was enlisted in the work. He visited Lanvin and Worth, Agnes and Patou, and others and induced them to use velvet in their gowns and hats. It was he who arranged for the distinguished Countess This or Duchess That to wear the hat or the gown. And as for the presentation of the idea to the public, the American buyer or the American woman of fashion was simply shown the velvet creations in the atelier of the dressmaker or the milliner. She bought the velvet because she liked it and because it was in fashion.

The editors of the American magazines and fashion reporters of the American newspapers likewise subjected to the actual (although created) circumstance, reflected it in their news, which, in turn, subjected the buyer and the consumer here to the same influences. The result was that what was at first a trickle of velvet became a flood. A demand was slowly, but deliberately, created in Paris and America. A big department store, aiming to be a style leader, advertised velvet gowns and hats on the authority of the French couturiers, and quoted original cables received from them. The echo of the new style was heard from hundreds of department stores throughout the country which wanted to be style leaders too. Bulletins followed dispatches. The mail followed the cables. And the American woman traveler appeared before the ship news photographers in velvet gown and hat.

The created circumstances had their effect. "Fickle fashion has veered to velvet," was one newspaper comment. And the industry in the United States again kept thousands busy.

The new propaganda, having regard to the constitution of society as a whole, not infrequently serves to focus and realize the desires of the masses. A desire for a specific reform, however widespread, cannot be translated into action until it is made articulate, and until it has exerted sufficient pressure upon the proper law-making bodies. Millions of housewives may feel that manufactured foods deleterious to health should be prohibited.

But there is little chance that their individual desires will be translated into effective legal form unless their half-expressed demand can be organized, made vocal, and concentrated upon the state legislature or upon the Federal Congress in some mode which will produce the results they desire. Whether they realize it or not, they call upon propaganda to organize and effectuate their demand. But clearly it is the intelligent minorities which need to make use of propaganda continuously and systematically. In the active proselytizing minorities in whom selfish interests and public interests coincide lie the progress and development of America. Only through the active energy of the intelligent few can the public at large become aware of and act upon new ideas.

Small groups of persons can, and do, make the rest of us think what they please about a given subject. But there are usually proponents and opponents of every propaganda, both of whom are equally eager to convince the majority.

*Why We Behave
Like Inhuman Beings*
(1949)

ONCE UPON A TIME—LONG, LONG ago in the fabulous 1920's—a noted American anthropologist, George Amos Dorsey, wrote a best-seller, *Why We Behave Like Human Beings*.

This appeared in the Coolidge Era, when the future looked boundlessly bright and everybody was going to win a prize in the national sweepstake of plenty. Prosperous, self-confident, hilariously optimistic, the U.S. was drinking bootleg liquor; dancing the Black Bottom; reading Hemingway, Cabell, and *Gentlemen Prefer Blondes*; cheering a young man named Lindbergh, who had just flown solo across the Atlantic; applauding *Marco Millions* by Eugene O'Neill, laughing at the satires of Sinclair Lewis and the antics of a new strip-cartoon character, Mickey Mouse.

The old American dream of rags to riches, log cabin to White House, was still going strong. Elbert Hubbard's *Message to Garcia* still inspired high school boys with the conviction that, if you let nothing stop you in the competitive obstacle race of our time, you were bound to reach the glittering goal of Success. Coue, a smiling Frenchman with a flare for semantics, had persuaded many Americans to recite, "Every day in every way I am growing better and better"; and millions believed this magic incantation would enable them to grab and keep forever the coveted brass ring as they whirled around on the golden merry-go-round of eternal prosperity. In the nationwide quest for fame and fortune just around the corner, thousands probed for the secret of it all in Bruce Barton's *The Man Nobody Knows*, which portrayed Christ as a super-salesman, town booster, and Rotary Club toastmaster.

America in those days was a world in which success was everybody's almost for the asking. All you had to do was work hard, brush your teeth with the right dentifrice, avoid B.O. and that nine-letter horror about which your best friends wouldn't tell you. Then you were sure to marry the boss's daughter, get a 20 per cent interest in the business, and live happily ever afterward in a land which had never heard of a housing shortage.

This sublime assurance pervaded even the highest levels. Concluding his story of the *Rise of American Civilization*, the late Charles A. Beard, dean of United States historians, announced in 1927 that this was the dawn of the gods. And from Washington, D. C., there emerged on history's horizon the shining promise of the Kellogg Pact, signed by the many nations which solemnly agreed to outlaw war and establish permanent world-wide peace. In this happy age men appeared to be quite human.

In the fall of 1929, this beautiful dream did a Humpty Dumpty. A historic process we had blandly ignored suddenly caught up with us, and woke us with a violent shock.

World War I had opened an epoch without precedent in history. Now, for over three decades, humanity has been rent asunder by uninterrupted conflict. Worldwide war, revolution, and counter-revolution have accompanied global depressions, national uprisings, class conflicts, conspiracies, putsches, underground resistance movements, civil war, dictatorship, fifth columns, show trials, assassinations, suicides, executions, and colonial revolts. Old empires have been destroyed; new nations have been created; republics have sprung up only to vanish under the boots of invading armies or totalitarian regimes.

The dream of universal prosperity, progress, and peace has been pulverized by universal ambition, violence, and fraud. No sooner is one aggressor beaten than another raises his mailed fist. Each war, worldwide or local, is followed by an ambiguous peace haunted by fear of the next war. Once kings battled with each other for the shape of things to come, then nations; now hemispheres and ideologies clash with conflicting promises and the force of modern armaments.

Never before has mankind undergone such vast changes in every aspect of its existence on so worldwide a scale, and the end is not yet in sight.

In the midst of this volcanic eruption of change, men have abandoned the religious and ethical conventions of forty centuries and have hounded each other to the grave with a ferocity which makes lions and tigers appear like harmless kittens. Large sections of the world have made "man's inhumanity to man" their fanatical creed, and deliberately employed the most bloodthirsty, paranoid cruelty to impose their will upon whole populations. Fuhrers, duces, caudillos, generalissimos, marshals, police states, gestapos, spies, informers, denouncers, accusers, unscrupulous propagandists, and totalitarian courts have played the grim overture to melodramas of history at whose climax appeared the firing squad; the hangman; the masked executioner with his silk hat and broadax; the concentration camp; the factory manned by slave labor; the incinerator where people were burned for their race, religion, or politics; the lamp shade faultlessly fashioned out of human skin.

For all its advanced democratic way of life, America has not wholly escaped the nightmare upheavals of this century. We have known depression, war, strikes, lynching, race riots, religious and racial bigotry, juvenile delinquency, increased divorce rates. And there has been an alarming rise in mental illness, the last desperate refuge of the acutely maladjusted from the tensions, dislocations, and horrors of an age which opened with a pistol shot at Sarajevo and ended its first act with the explosion of the bomb at Hiroshima.

In the dawn of the modern world, Shakespeare could exclaim: "What a piece of work is man! how noble in reason! how infinite in faculty! in form and moving how express and adorable! in action how like an angel! in apprehension how like a god!" Today we are less impressed by man's angelic and divine equalities. Rather, we are overwhelmed by the discovery that, under pressure, millions of people can so easily succumb to mechanized headhunting and cannibalism. And so the current $64 question is not why we behave like human beings, but why we behave like *inhuman* beings.

Everybody is asking this question, from the man in the street to the most learned scientist, for the vents and discoveries of the past four decades have forced us to change our basic viewpoints about ourselves and the world we live in.

The pioneer discoveries of the nineteenth century science encouraged the belief that man's unbroken progress and freedom lay wholly in mastering the physical world. Every accelerating invention, unloosed by the Industrial Revolution, seemed to guarantee not only universal well-being, but universal peace. Today, when the physical sciences have perfected aircraft that travel at the speed of sound, and promise to release us from the control of gravitation, the material conquest of nature is at the highest peak in history. Yet the world is aflame with conflict rendered all the more violent and devastating by the inventions of science.

This has altered the emphasis of science itself. It is not surprising that religious conferences, such as those which met recently at Lambeth and Amsterdam, should call for moral regeneration as man's last best hope on earth. Nor is it surprising that a congress of the world's leading psychiatrists, meeting about the same time in London, should urge the study and control of man's nature, especially his aggressive impulses, as the major solution of the twentieth century crisis. It is logical, too, that a social scientist like Dr Hornell Hart of Duke University, winner of the Edward L. Bernays Atomic Energy Award for action-related research in the social implications of atomic energy, should propose a "Manhattan Project" of the Social Sciences as the first step toward grappling realistically with the crisis of which man is the center.

But of late we have had unexpected news of the man-bites-dog variety. Now it is the *physical* scientists themselves who have begun to emphasize man, about whom we know so little, rather than nature, which we have mastered so well that it may destroy us unless we learn to master ourselves.

Speaking at this year's convention of the American Association for the Advancement of Science, its president, Dr. Edmund W. Sinnott of Yale University, said: "Man, not nature, is the great problem today. These vast new powers in the hands of selfish or arrogant men simply increase their power to dominate their fellows." Man wants to be much more than a well-kept beast, Doctor Sinnott said, adding: "Unless we give him ample opportunity and encouragement to cultivate the higher side of his nature fully and can free him from the restraints of dogma and compulsion, he will never be satisfied and there will be no real hope for him."

At the same convention, Dr. Roger J. Williams, noted Texas University biochemist, said that while scientists have learned a great deal about the atom of matter, they are still profoundly ignorant about the atom of society, the human individual, a much more explosive force than the atom bomb. "Civilization," Professor Williams said, "is not threatened by atomic bombs and biological warfare today. It is threatened by ourselves. If civilization goes down, man will be his own undoing. The instruments and tools that he uses will not be the source of the trouble."

The key problem of the twentieth century is one of human relations. The continued triumphs of physics, chemistry, and biology are taken for granted. But if we want to know why, in the midst of these triumphs of mind over matter, we continue to behave like inhuman beings and how, in spite of everything, we can learn to behave like human beings, we must turn to the new sciences which have begun their real development only in the past thirty years—anthropology, psychiatry, psychoanalysis, and sociology.

This makes me feel somewhat at home, because my uncle, Sigmund Freud, pointed out long ago that the solution of most of our problems lies in following out scientifically Socrates' famous injunction: *Know thyself!* Today it is recognized psychiatric treatment for the maladjusted to cure themselves by knowing themselves. Since man as a whole seems to be maladjusted to the new conditions imposed by the twentieth century, this technique is being applied to man as a whole.

In their attempt to discover why we behave as we do, the sciences are probing the nature of man from various angles. Physiologically, the human being is the way his body works; psychologically, the way his mind works; sociologically, the way he functions in groups; biologically, the ways he reacts to heredity and environment; pedagogically, the way he is formed by early and adult education; economically, as the beneficiary or the victim of our mass production system. By exploring these phases of everybody's behavior, we may come up with answers which may explain some mysteries of human nature and conduct. This fundamental knowledge may help us find the way to better social adjustment and happiness.

The various sciences now agree that societies are stable and healthy when individuals obtain the physical, intellectual, emotional, esthetic, moral, and religious satisfactions which their natures require. One of the reasons why we behave like inhuman beings is that so many people throughout the world are frustrated in their basic needs and desires. Severe frustration tends to throw people back to primitive and infantile modes of conduct. It rouses fear, and fear rouses a desire for revenge. Above all, frustrations, in a world raging with unremitting conflict, stimulate the aggressive impulses which a satisfying civilization sublimates into constructive channels.

Recently there has been a great deal of discussion among scientists about man's aggressive impulses. Dr. Thomas Nixon Carver of Harvard has classified aggressive forms of conduct as destructive, deceptive, and persuasive.

Destructive forms include war, robbery, duelling, murder, and brawling; deceptive forms are thieving, swindling, adulteration of goods, false advertising; persuasive aggression involves political, erotic, commercial, and legal attacks upon others. No matter how we classify it, aggression always seeks to bring injury or death to others; and these days the question, "Why do we behave like inhuman beings?" has become "Why do we behave aggressively?"

The opening in 1914 of this age of blood and blunder came as a terrible shock to a generation which had absorbed only at the top intellectual level the real meaning of Darwin's theory of evolution, and had no real grasp of historic time. Even today many do not understand the fundamental concept of modern science that human beings are descended from lower forms of animal life; and that, like other animals, we seek to satisfy our desire and defend ourselves against danger.

The basic desires and fears are there, but with the development of civilization, we learn to control them in the interests of group survival. Indeed, civilization begins with man's renunciation and sublimation of jungle impulses. Family and social life are impossible unless men curb their primitive sex and aggressive instincts. Even the most primitive societies prohibit incest, robbery, and murder. When these prohibitions break down, we get anarchy. When they are abandoned by a despotic ruling elite, we get a totalitarian state with the law of jungle imposed on a helpless slave population. On the other hand, when the repression of primitive impulses is carried too far, we get first hypocrisy, then widespread frustration and neurosis.

Modern science is looking for the factors in man which can make for balanced individuals and a balanced society which recognizes the force of man's primitive impulses and converts them into a source of creative power; or at least mitigates their destructiveness.

More and more the modern psychiatrist tends to relate the contemporary crisis to our early childhood experience in the family and society. People are not static units. Like everything else in the world, they evolve and change under the pressure of circumstance. As the world makes them, so they make the world. Civilization requires that each of us adjust himself to social living. When faulty upbringing or makeup prevents us from making this necessary adjustment, we behave like inhuman beings.

We do so because even the oldest civilizations on record go back only 6,000 years—a mere drop in the millions of years since man emerged from the unit cell. We were jungle animals far, far longer than we have been civilized men, and the impulses of the jungle animal lie dormant in our being beneath the surface of civilization.

When we come into the world as children, our impulses are those of primitive creatures struggling for survival in the primitive animal world. The psychological problems of childhood revolve around the need for becoming socially adjusted to family, community, country, and world. All education and training—at home, school, and church—is directed toward curbing the primitive impulses, especially those of aggression with which we are born, and redirecting them to social ends.

But those who bring us up, above all our parents, are not always aware that if their attempts to civilize us are indifferent, ignorant, or brutal, if they fail to take into account the particular needs of our developing personality, we may become frustrated. Creative redirection of the child's primitive impulses is one thing; the suppression which comes from lack of love and understanding quite another. Flowers that fester are far worse than weeds, Shakespeare observed; and natural impulses which fester through repression may emerge in later life as impotent neurosis or dangerous aggression. If we are brought up as inhuman beings we are likely to become inhuman beings. Nobody is so cruel in adult life as the man who was weaned on cruelty.

It is not only in the family, however, that aggression can be encouraged by aggressive upbringing. Society is that larger family which brings all of us up. Its failure to do so properly can also sour and inflame primitive impulses which ought to be sublimated and redirected constructively. The child who is humiliated on account of his poverty, race, religion, or looks may harbor feelings of vengeance which, in a violent age like ours, are likely to find aggressive outlets.

Man lives not by bread alone, the Bible tells us. The child, father of the man, needs love. He needs to feel that he is accepted and cherished by his family and community. If he is rejected—above all *unjustly* rejected—the iron enters his soul and he becomes embittered, vindictive, and aggressive.

In this epoch of worldwide dislocation and conflict, frustrated people often take out their aggression in antisocial behavior. They try to soothe their own psychological wounds by wounding others through racial and religious discrimination and persecution of so-called inferior peoples.

Anatole France once said that Napoleon overran the world

with blood because he was a failure in his own tent; and modern psychologists have found that the men who murdered millions in concentration camps were seeking scapegoats for the forgotten suffering and frustration of their childhood. The child who is economically and psychologically insecure, who eats his crust of bread in tears and feels that he is rejected and unloved, is likely to develop into the man who seeks a "whipping boy" whom he will force to pay for his early defeats.

Science is giving a great deal of thought to the fact that so many of our modern political sadists, from the most obscure brownshirt to the booming dictator at the top, are psychological cripples devoured by hate and resentment which goes back to early childhood.

Frustration, defeat, suffering, insecurity, and the sense of being one of the "insulted and injured," are very dangerous things during times of economic, political, and military insecurity.

It is, we have discovered to our cost, only too easy for the psychological monster with a flair for leadership to promise a heaven of security and victory on earth, and thus rouse primitive impulses of aggression in millions of frustrated people.

A paranoid like Hitler had no trouble inflaming a German people smarting under a lost war and a harsh peace, or to intoxicate them with the promise of world conquest into behaving like inhuman beings on a colossal scale. Here, as everywhere else today, barbarous aggression was mistaken for a short cut to achievement, and destruction as a short cut to a sense of psychological security.

Another reason why we behave like inhuman beings is sociological. We live in a highly competitive society. Our behavior in this society is predicated on jungle rules of survival.

As civilization, morality, and ethics developed in the course of history, men drew up rules of the game which tend to make us behave more like human beings. But modern competitive society is still so relatively new that these rules are not as well defined as they ought to be, and we do not adhere to them as much as we might. The pecuniary values of competitive society make us punish adultery, which affects the happiness of three people, far more harshly than adulteration, which may affect the health of millions.

It is true, as many of our wisest social scientists point out, that environment is a far more powerful factor in shaping our behavior than heredity. For the most part, we are what our surroundings make us. Just as the child in its mother's womb begins as an embryo and passes through the various stages of man's evolution from the unit cell, so each of us has to learn in his own lifetime the entire heritage of the race in our particular civilization. William Graham Sumner—from whom Franklin D. Roosevelt got the phrase "The Forgotten Man"— calls this heritage our folkways. In essence, this heritage comes to us through our environment. Our folkways are the everyday incidents of our environment which pattern our thoughts and actions.

Some individuals absorb these patterns more quickly and easily than others. Some have little or no capacity to absorb them. These regress easily to the primitive folkways of the jungle which are part of our unconscious heritage.

Another factor in our environment which makes this regression possible is that of the two billion inhabitants of the world, one-half are still illiterate. Unequipped to absorb the gains of civilization, they are responsive not to the wisdom of the ages, but to words, pictures, and actions as these would be interpreted by primitive man. They are easy prey for distortion and superstition. Instead of being guided by knowledge and understanding, they are driven by the most primitive fears and hopes.

According to the 1940 census, the average American adult has had only eight years of education. He lives in a highly complex world of competitive drives where all sorts of conflicting appeals, representing diverse interests, are made to the public day in and day out.

This leaves the door open for the conscious or unconscious propagation of anti-social, primitive viewpoints. Those who are not educated to resist the onslaught succumb to words and pictures whose explosive meanings stimulate the inhuman behavior which is the stock in trade of bigotry, fanaticism, and the fantasy of world conquest.

To be sure, we have in this country a system of public education which, as the Educational Policies Commission recently put it, should educate men to be free citizens in a free democracy. But there is a great gap between this ideal and the reality around us. The National Education Association and similar groups have shown that many states, cities, counties, and villages lack the physical equipment, the properly trained teachers, and the basic ideas to fit the child for life today and tomorrow.

To climax this serious lag, our educational system does not carry into the schoolroom all that the social sciences have discovered about human nature and conduct. Children are still taught antiquated ideas by antiquated methods. When the adolescent leaves school, he is often ill prepared to meet the complex problems of modern life. In most cases he has been fitted for an entirely different pattern of life, one much closer to the nineteenth than the twentieth century.

This may give him a sense of psychological insecurity. He may feel let down and resentful because those who had charge of his education dropped him into the seething contemporary world unequipped to meet it. If he meets defeat and frustration in his struggle for security or success, he becomes the perfect sucker for the paranoid demagogue with his dazzling, unscrupulous promises of revenge, conquest, and plunder that will include all the good and evil things of which the frustrated, anonymous man feels himself deprived.

All these factors which make us behave like inhuman beings are augmented by the great paradox of the twentieth century. We have made fabulous progress in technology without comparable progress in the ability to handle human relations.

We can make the atom bomb, but do not know how to control it socially so that it does not annihilate most of mankind.

We can press a button and start a TVA powerhouse, yet cannot prevent race riots caused by ignorance, misunderstanding, and prejudice.

We are so elated over our mastery of the machine that, like the characters in Samuel Butler's satire, we run the danger of ceasing to be men. And though we know perfectly well how fatal another armed conflict may be for the whole of civilization, there has never been so much talk of war as now, only a few years after two wars to end all war.

That is why all the sciences today, from psychoanalysis to physics, are concerned with the problem of why we behave like inhuman beings. It is symptomatic of these times that the staff of the United Nations has its own psychiatric consultant.

Assuming this post, Dr. Carl F. Sulzberger of the New York Postgraduate School and Hospital urged further study of mankind with the hope that someday men will not have to fight an enemy, real or imaginary, to get along in the world.

Psychiatry, he said, is definitely on the way to acquiring an understanding of human behavior that may someday aid in achieving peace. The key to many current problems of human behavior is the study of the child's frustration and disappointments, since "the pattern of anxiety and satisfactions that will later color the whole life is established at an early age."

It is also a sign of the times that Dr. Carl Binger of Cornell University, addressing the recent International Mental Health Congress in London, urged statesmen and politicians, who would not think of waging war without the help of scientists, to give scientists a hearing on how to prevent wars. Doctor Binger confirmed Freud's thesis that wars result from man's aggressive instincts, and he equated war with ailments having no single cause, but several causes, all contributing to the final catastrophe.

Thus science, with its modern equipment of experiment and method, is seeking to solve the problem of inhuman behavior through greater and greater knowledge of man and the world in which he lives. The key to our liberation from our jungle heritage of force and fraud lies in accelerated self-understanding. The truth shall indeed make us free when we learn, with the same control we exercise over physical nature, that it must now be the truth about *ourselves*.

An Educational
Program for Unions
(1947)

PUBLIC OPINION ON MOST IMPORTANT ISSUES goes through a process of evolution. The public at first sees only a small part of any issue, just as only the top of an iceberg is visible. Then as the result of educational activities, people are gradually induced to see more and more until they get a full view of the subject—they see not only the peak but the larger submerged part of the iceberg.

In an analogous way, the whole problem of industrial relations is highly visible today. The educational efforts of unions have been an important factor in forcing the issue out into the open.

In this article I am going to discuss industrial relations from the public relations standpoint. I have had a good deal of experience in day-to-day contact with these problems. I have made a study of business and public attitudes to labor and labor attitudes to business. I have studied union educational programs.

It appears to me that unions still have an important job of work to do; namely, to carry on an intensified factual educational campaign, to instruct not only the general public and management, but their own union members as well, on the bedrock facts of the struggle for industrial democracy.

All of us want and expect a better life, a better hometown, a better America, with security and employment for all.

We have not succeeded yet. There are violent disagreements and conflict on how to get the better life. We are bedeviled by psychological and economic insecurities. Cynicism, disillusionment, and frustration undermine our morale. We have turned our aggressions against our own people instead of a common enemy. America is a battlefield for ideological and group struggles: white versus Negro; native-born versus foreign; management versus labor. We must take positive action against these internal dissensions, just as we are trying to take positive action against international war.

The most important of these internal struggles is between management and labor. Industrial peace can be reached only if we go after it intelligently. Labor and management can plan and work together to realize the goals of our society. Punitive legislation won't solve our problems—the answer is education in industrial relations. The public, the employer, and the worker must know what it is all about.

Labor should assume part of this responsibility for education. What can the educational directors of the large unions do to lick this problem?

It is essentially a public relations problem. People must want cleanliness before they buy soap. They must want higher education before they swarm to the colleges. In the same way people must want unions before they are willing to support specific union goals. A public that understands what unions have done for the good of the country is going to be more open-minded and friendly to union programs. If the public does not understand the value of unions, it will be guided by prejudice, untruths, and distortions.

Let us examine one progressive union's educational program and see whether it starts in at the foundation and builds up. The program follows several broad lines:

First, the union educates its members to enter fully into the union's work; to develop effective and mature leadership for handling bargaining problems; to strengthen democracy within the organization; to build union solidarity. Through these activities the union tries to reach its goals—higher real wages, industry-wide wage agreements, wage equalization, a guaranteed annual wage, equality for women workers.

Second, the union tries to strengthen democracy in a number of ways. It fights inflation. It encourages union activity in civic and political matters, in co-operation with farmers, consumers, and others. It works for better housing, assistance to veterans, health programs, and civil liberties.

The third part of its program, not announced but well understood, is a matter of "selling" itself to its own rank and file. (Research, advertising, and public relations men in industry have the same problem. The client wants immediate visible results.)

As I study the union's educational activities, it seems to me that it might undertake three additional programs of education, so that the public will understand what the union wants and why, and be more willing to accept its goals.

1. Make the public understand the value to the country of sound unions and mature union leadership.

2. Make the employer understand the value of unions to him, and make him realize that he needs to apply the science of humanics, the study of human relations.

3. Make the worker understand our industrial system and his role in it.

This type of education will lay the foundations for a broader understanding of controversial economic issues, and build toward increased co-operation between labor and the other major sectors of our society.

That there is an acute need for labor to educate the public has been demonstrated in many ways. Authoritative polls again and again reveal large areas of ignorance on the subject of industrial relations. For example, more than a quarter of the people asked were unable to answer intelligently this question put by an Elmo Roper *Fortune* poll late in 1946: "Suppose you had been acting as a referee in labor-management disputes during the past three months; do you think your decisions would probably have been more often in favor of labor's side or more often in favor of management's side?"

The major reason for the American public's ignorance of matters concerning labor is its lack of factual information. The public receives its impressions of unions mainly from newspaper headlines or radio broadcasts, usually just before or in the midst of a time of controversy. Neither a union nor a management point-of-view expressed during controversy helps much to clarify; on the contrary, it merely intensifies existing attitudes. People are more receptive to facts when issues are not superheated by emotional pressures.

Most people, I would say, do not know that unions have increased purchasing power and profits as well as wages, that they have been responsible for adjustments in our industrial system that have raised our standards of living. The public has little idea of what an extension of unionism might mean to our whole economy. It does not know what the advantages of unions are. It is unaware of what can be learned from the experiences of other countries. The public really does not know why some unions engage in harmful practices and others not. It has little knowledge of how the democratic process operates within unions.

The 1944 CIO constitution says at one point that the unions' objectives are to find "means to establish peaceful relations with their employers ... to protect and extend our democratic institutions and civil rights and liberties and thus to perpetuate the cherished tradition of our democracy." These are aims that all Americans can and will support—if they have the facts and the knowledge on which to base their judgments. They will not have the facts unless someone makes a planned campaign to provide them. Progressive unions are in a position to do this. They can give the public the following kinds of information about unions:

1. What is a union?

   How does it function? Give the basic story of union organization, its history, and development. Explain the structure and internal government of unions; the different kinds of unions, industrial and craft; local, national, and international; affiliated and unaffiliated. Explain clearly the facts about jurisdiction, the methods by which officers are chosen, and their duties, membership dues, and disposition of union finances.

2. What are the educational and welfare activities of unions?
   Cover the story of the labor press and its function. Publicize the educational activities and benefit programs of unions such as vocational training, apprenticeship methods, labor

banking, insurance, and the like.

3. What are the facts about collective bargaining?

   Explain this little-understood term; tell what the process actually is, what takes place, how agreements are reached.

4. What are the facts about labor disputes in general?

   How do they arise? What are the principal reasons for disputes? Are there as many as the public has been led to believe?

5. What do the words mean?

   No small part of this campaign would be to define many of the terms commonly used in labor-management discussions, but only vaguely understood by the public. A whole vocabulary needs translating. Only a small percentage of the public knows the distinction of meanings among wages, wage awards, wage practices, wage differentials, and wage stabilization; workload, work restriction, and work sharing; the closed shop, the union shop, and the open shop.

Our second proposal is that the unions educate the employer on the subject of unions and human relations. It can teach the employer by the same methods it uses with the public.

Today, while it is generally recognized that more employers than formerly are ready to accept their social responsibility, this is by no means true of all of them. According to a recent *Fortune* poll, more than ninety per cent of management thinks management has a definite responsibility beyond the sphere of profits; but a third of those queried stated that they believe only one fourth or less of management possesses such social consciousness. In other words, management itself does not believe it has fulfilled its social responsibilities.

Industry must overhaul its thinking. Its use of the physical sciences, of technology, has far outstripped its use of the science of social behavior—of how to work together.

Industry is not merely "business," it is a social institution as well. Industrial management requires skill in group relations. In the common interest unions should help teach management how to work intelligently with labor.

Some difficulty in industry is caused by the Victorian attitudes of certain employers, who want to get back the hold on workers they feel they have lost because of workers' loyalty to unions. They resent and fear unions. They fail to educate their company officials on how to work with people. Some do not understand that the worker, as Philip Murray put it so succinctly, is faced with "the primary human problem of earning a living."

But the worker also wants more than just a job, and many employers do not yet realize this. Elmo Roper showed, by authoritative polling some years ago, "that in the order of their importance to him, the average American wants a sense of security, an opportunity to advance, to be treated like a human being rather than as a number on the payroll, a sense of human dignity that comes from feeling that his work is useful to society as a whole." These preferences were again confirmed by more recent polls. About half of those asked said they would pick a job that pays quite a low income but which they were sure of keeping. About one quarter said they wanted a job which pays a good income but which they have a fifty-fifty chance of losing. Still fewer said they preferred a job which pays an extremely high income if you make the grade but in which you lose almost everything if you don't.

Disruptions in labor-management relations arise from many reasons other than wage disputes. They arise from a continuous sense of insecurity, from real or apparent managerial unfairness in adjusting contractual relations, from the harmful effects of assembly line work, and from work and pay scales planned on an individual instead of a group basis.

In many cases, these causes of worker dissatisfaction stem directly from preconceived employer attitudes. Educational directors of a great union can help to alter these attitudes by means of an educational program aimed at the employer, such as the following:

1. Educate employers to the place of unions in our system.
2. Acquaint employers with the data on human relations that have been gathered by universities, labor unions, foundations, and such groups as the Society for the Psychological Study of Social Issues, the Society for the Advancement of Management, and the American Academy of Political and Social Science.
3. Persuade employers to stimulate further research by industrial relations schools such as those at Cornell, Princeton, and Harvard.
4. Encourage employers to carry on technological research to improve working conditions.
5. Help management to develop new approaches to the industrial relations problem. Stabilized employment, which some organizations have found enormously

beneficial, is an example.

6. Point up the importance of intelligent, honest, unbiased industrial relations personnel.

7. Urge management to encourage responsible leadership among the unions.

8. Urge employers to support housing projects, minimum wage legislation, social security, and other programs to strengthen democracy.

When I speak of educational efforts aimed at management, I know the idea is not new. It has been tried, sometimes with decidedly negative results. Unions have had disillusioning experiences in their attempts to persuade management to consider the union point-of-view, and unions may feel that anyone who suggests educating management is probably starry-eyed.

Management's principal fear is that if it allows labor the right to advise, labor will somehow gain complete control. Efforts to dispel this belief cannot succeed overnight; but just as the displacement of one log can break up a log jam, the winning over of one man may win over others.

The educational process builds new points of view by continuous and repeated efforts. There are innumerable ways of reaching the attention of employers. Unions can arrange for speaking engagements before employer groups, trade associations, chambers of commerce, boards of trade, and such groups as the Lions and the Rotary Clubs; radio talks and speeches at public meetings will carry the message. People can be educated by word of mouth in conversation. A thought clearly expressed has a way of starting a chain reaction. Unions can reach employers by the printed word—by sending clear, factual stories to newspapers and other publications, by advertisements, pamphlets, and broadsides, by using all the communications media. Intelligently written letters addressed to top management will be read; talks by union executives to community groups reported in the newspapers will get attention; material prepared for special groups in the community, such as women's clubs, lawyers, the clergy, will indirectly affect the businessman. Unions can enlist the support of colleges, foundations, progressive employers, consumer and other groups.

No approach should be overlooked in carrying forward one's program. Workers have a duty to the common good to help educate one of the most potent groups in America—management.

The third activity I propose is to educate union members in economics. Many reliable polls have proved the need of such education. For example, recent surveys of cross-sections of factory workers by the magazine *Factory Management* revealed that more than half of the workers queried had no opinion as to which top union leader is the most effective in getting better wages, hours, and working conditions. About one third had no opinion on whether the prices a company charges for its products are too high, not high enough, or about right. About one third had no opinion on their bosses' pay. About half had no opinion on whether dividends were too high or too low.

Few people, let alone workers, know much about the technical problems of business finance. Without such knowledge, however, the worker is handicapped when engaged in bargaining. But if the worker understands management's problems, he can bargain on a realistic basis. Some well-informed unions actually come to the aid of management when it is in financial difficulties, as the Amalgamated Clothing Workers have done, because they know that such assistance directly benefits everyone dependent on the particular industry.

Unions such as the Amalgamated have been able to take drastic steps of this kind only because their membership have been educated to appreciate the value of mutual assistance. This education had been accomplished over a long period of years by the union itself. What the Amalgamated does, other unions can do.

Walter Reuther has said that "the test of democratic trade unionism in a democratic society must be its willingness to lead the fight for the welfare of the whole community." Management has the same obligation.

Organized labor can help educate both management and workers to a realization of this obligation. Such education has one basic purpose: to create understanding, so that management and labor may work together effectively and prevent clashes. And this co-operation must come, for our system cannot stand continuous warfare.

HUMAN ENGINEERING AND SOCIAL ADJUSTMENT (1979)

REVOLUTIONS IN TECHNOLOGY, TRANSPORTATION, AND communications of the last century continue today. They have brought and continue to bring us closer to the One World Wendell Willkie envisaged. No longer is anyone anywhere an island unto himself. We are all part of a whole, getting closer to each other all the time. Practically, the world is one room. Adjustments of individuals and groups to one another become a necessity, the order of the day. Some use the expressions "dependence" and "interdependence" to describe today's situation. Peaceful co-existence is the great desideratum. Adjustment must take place between all in the society, between nations and nations, groups and groups, individuals and individuals, between seller and buyer, between all members of the society.

The revolutions that brought us all closer together have brought with them increased literacy. That has brought people into greater participation in all activities of the society. This has also increased "people power" and its importance to all elements of the society.

Adjustment of groups and individuals with each other is brought about by their actions and the words they use to project their actions. Word symbols play an ancillary role to action in aiding the process of adjustment. They develop understanding that produces socially responsible action by those exposed to them. They also bring understanding to those affected by action.

Actions and words resolve potential conflict in the society and bring about adjustments. In the public interest, maladjustments between groups and groups, individuals and individuals, individuals and groups must be eliminated wherever they exist. Maladjustments may be due to ignorance, prejudice, or the apathy of those who carry out actions that affect others. Force, threat, and intimidation have no place in our society. Socially responsible action helps to bring about adjustment. So does the use of word symbols that bring about understanding. We may call such processes communication, education, persuasion, propaganda, proselytism, teaching. Whatever the name, we must try to avoid maladjustment and conflict. There are strategies and tactics of bringing about adjustment that have been found effective in wide areas of activity. We have called the process of bringing about such adjustment "the engineering of consent."

The network of communication in our society is extensive and complex. Obviously it does not come into play in matters that concern limited publics and limited areas. But where it does, the extensive and complex network of communications in this country needs to be taken into consideration. And this network is so extensive that it demands an engineering approach to cope with it; hence the term, "engineering of consent." We would waste time and effort and whatever else we put into the attempts at adjustment unless we adopted such an approach.

Here are some examples of the complex network of

communication. The Federal Communication Commission figures show these television outlets in the United States: 513 VHF commercial television stations, 196 UHF commercial television stations, 95 VHF educational stations, and 155 UHF educational stations. Ninety-seven point seven per cent of the 73 million households in the United States have televisions. In addition, there are 4459 AM commercial radio stations, 2752 FM commercial stations, and 799 FM educational stations.

A breakdown of the print media indicates that 127 million Americans read magazines. There are 1762 daily newspapers in the country, 7530 weekly newspapers, 2400 trade publications. The circulation of morning daily newspapers is, according to the latest figures, 25,858,386. Evening circulation is 35,118,625. There are college and university newspapers, foreign language newspapers, and special service newspapers on topics from agriculture to sports.

And this listing does not include the books, hardback and soft cover, published in a year. Nor the billboards, circulars, and other forms of advertising that seek public attention and support for what they espouse. Nor does it list the person-to-person, word-of-mouth contacts between people, or the uses of the lecture platform. One estimate places at over 400 impacts a day the attempt in one way or another to bring about a coincidence of attitude and action between projector of idea and public.

The process of engineering of consent, as we call it, is based on the Jeffersonian thesis that consent or adjustment is the basic underlying concept on which the well-being of the society rests. The individual member of the democratic society gives his consent to what goes on in the society and brings about an adjusted society. This holds for non-profit and for-profit organizations, for products, ideas, and services that need public support for their viability. In engineering of consent both actions and words play a role. But actions speak louder than words. Words occupy a secondary role. Unless actions are in the public interest, words in the long run fail. And adjustment fails. Historians after World War I, referring to President Woodrow Wilson, wrote that words won the war and lost the peace. This truth is universal and applies to all activity aimed at engineering the consent of the public at the highest level of adjustment.

The engineering of consent is marked by eight principles that apply to all problems of enlisting public interest and support to reach top adjustment goals. Here they are:

1. Define your goals.
2. Research your publics by public opinion and/or market research.
3. Reorient your goals if necessary, to ensure that they are realistic and attainable in the light of your research.
4. Determine your strategy—how and when you will use your four M's—mindpower, manpower, mechanics, and money—to meet your goals of highest possible adjustment.
5. Reorient your goals to ensure that they are realistic and attainable, in the light of your research.
6. Determine the organization necessary to carry out your goals.
7. Time and plan your tactics.
8. Make up a budget.

Your goals need to be defined in three time periods.

Determination of a longtime goal is an essential first step. This longtime goal may be defined in terms of the attitudes and actions expected of your publics in X number of years. They may also be defined in terms of the tangibles you expect in the same number of years: if you are a corporation, not only the percentage of business you expect to get in your particular field, but the number and type of customers, employees, outlets or whatever—even the number of stockholders, if you are publicly held. Naturally, goals will vary with the kind of activity being considered. So will the number of years for which goals are set. An educational institution of higher learning can set goals for a longer period than a business enterprise in the field of science and invention. The number of years varies with different conditions. The more specific your goals, the more valuable the public opinion and/or market research will be.

After the research has been completed, it will be possible to set the two other essential goals, the immediate and the intermediate goal. The immediate goal might be a year or so away, the intermediate goal several years.

Public opinion and/or market research, the next step, applies the findings of modern-day social sciences to the problems at hand. Modern day research in this area defines and isolates areas of public interest and support, markets, and the like. It isolates and defines the motives and attitudes of the publics concerned towards the particular service, product, idea, or individual or group. It defines public areas of potential interest. It indicates accurately potentials of success. It enables the maker of the survey to identify present favorable attitudes as a basis for intensification, to convert attitudes on the fence to favorable attitudes and action, and tells him how to eliminate negative attitudes.

The research also indicates whether the original goal set is realistic or unrealistic and the extent to which it is either. If the research shows the unrealism of goals, they can be reoriented. Scientific surveys require that they be made by highly trained, skilled professional pollsters or market research professionals. The need for them has been met by the Gallups, Harrises, Ropers, and other experts. But their availability does not preclude the layman without the funds to retain them from going ahead. There are numerous good books on polling that should help the layman to plan and carry out a poll by himself. Any poll intelligently planned and carried out, as a basis for procedure, is sounder than proceeding without a poll of any kind.

Research will also reveal and identify the opinion molders and group leaders who play an important role in affecting public attitudes and public attitudes to the project at issue. Opinion molders are those who through the spoken and written word have built constituencies of their own, whose judgments and actions they affect. Opinion molders of course reflect their constituencies' attitudes. They also affect them. Opinion molders may often be the short cut to the publics you desire to adjust with.

Then there are the group leaders. They are the elected or selected leaders of the interest groups and group interests that make up our society. From the President of the United States to the president of the local union, from the president of the Federation of Women's Clubs to the bishop or cardinal, they play a role in affecting the attitudes and actions of their constituencies. They all play their parts in the engineering of consent.

Reorientation of goals will follow if the research indicates the original goals are unrealistic. Goals may have represented simply fulfilled desires instead of realistic appraisal. Reorientation of goals makes it possible also to make a decision on immediate and intermediate goals. It should be kept in mind that research may reveal that, to meet the longtime goal, the sequence of events may not necessarily be logical. Illogical sequences may lead to ultimate goals.

Strategy determination indicates how you will use your resources to meet your objectives, i.e., in what proportions and with what timing you will use the four M's available—mindpower, manpower, mechanics, and money.

Effectiveness of your strategy depends on your professional know-how, the application of art to a science. Strategy will decide whether your action will be a slow process of education, a blitzkrieg, whatever. Many strategies available offer a choice in determining a course of action. Research will aid in the formulation of strategy.

The themes and appeals you will use in bringing about top adjustment with your publics depend in great part on your research. The researcher will discover what aspects of your venture appeal to what publics. Your themes will appeal to basic motivations—a desire to be a leader or a follower, a desire for immortality or for parental love, and a host of others.

The timing and planning of tactics comprise all the actions you will undertake, from changing certain attitudes and actions to conform with the public interest to contacts with your publics through the media and opinion molders. This timing and planning of tactics will result in a blueprint for each of the three time periods (immediate, intermediate, and long term) and will indicate what you will do and when. It will show the action and attitude changes research indicated you should undertake.

The complexity of the network of communications has already been pointed out. Obviously an attempt should be made to use all that reach your publics.

In this connection, the overt act, the created circumstances built around your idea, may well be helpful in gaining visibility with your publics through relevant media. Celebration of the two hundredth anniversary of the United States by our government was such an overt act. It was a conscious effort by our government to make the people realize the values of their system. To be sure it was poorly conceived and carried out, but still it reached many members of the public. Wilson's "Fourteen Points" demonstrates this concept, as do the "Four Freedoms" of Roosevelt. They are conscious efforts to bring about adjustment.

But words by themselves make little impact unless they reflect acceptable action or are associated with concepts that give them strength. Social scientists have found that people accept only what they *a priori* are willing to accept. Unless words reflect factual evidence, authority, reason, tradition, or carry strong emotion they lose their impact on individuals who *a priori* do not believe what they convey.

It must also be remembered that in our society the meaning of words is as fragile as a soap bubble or lace. If we want to gain acceptance for our words, they must reflect acceptable concepts and be reinforced in their meaning by associating them with the elements of acceptance just referred to.

The last item is making a budget. Money is an essential element in any activity because mechanics cost money. Manpower and mind- power often are available to carry on activities. Planning for the expenditures necessary in any activity of this kind is essential. When mindpower and manpower are not available these expenditures must be taken into consideration and advance planning made for them. It should be kept in mind that for nonprofit activities that serve the public interest, mindpower and manpower can often be found on a basis of contribution to the effort.

Advance budgeting is indicated, in any case.

It should be added that, in our society, all human activities are subject to abuse. Antisocial individuals in old and respected professions deviate from professional codes of conduct, in law and medicine and other professions. But the integrity of the profession and its practice remain. Obviously, the actions described in this piece may be and sometimes are abused. There are demagogues not only in politics, but in all branches of endeavor. Truth and ethical conduct continue despite them.

In our complex society, an engineering approach to bring adjustment at the highest level is essential to the society's well-being.

FROM
*CRYSTALLIZING PUBLIC
OPINION*
(1923)

PART I

CHAPTER II

THE PUBLIC RELATIONS COUNSEL; THE INCREASED AND INCREASING IMPORTANCE OF THE PROFESSION

THE RISE OF THE MODERN PUBLIC relations counsel is based on the need for and the value of his services. Perhaps the most significant social, political and industrial fact about the present century is the increased attention which is paid to public opinion, not only by individuals, groups or movements that are dependent on public support for their success, but also by men and organizations which until very recently stood aloof from the general public and were able to say, "The public be damned."

The public today demands information and expects also to be accepted as judge and jury in matters that have a wide public import. The public, whether it invests its money in subway or railroad tickets, in hotel rooms or restaurant fare, in silk or soap, is a highly sophisticated body. It asks questions, and if the answer in word or action is not forthcoming or satisfactory, it turns to other sources for information or relief.

The willingness to spend thousands of dollars in obtaining professional advice on how best to present one's views or products to a public is based on this fact.

On every side of American life, whether political, industrial, social, religious or scientific, the increasing pressure of public judgment has made itself felt. Generally speaking, the relationship and interaction of the public and any movement is rather obvious. The charitable society which depends upon voluntary contributions for its support has a clear and direct interest in being favorably represented before the public. In the same way, the great corporation which is in danger of having its profits taxed away or its sales fall off or its freedom impeded by legislative action must have recourse to the public to combat successfully these menaces. Behind these obvious phenomena, however, lie three recent tendencies of fundamental importance; first, the tendency of small organizations to aggregate into groups of such size and importance that the public tends to regard them as semi-public services; second, the increased readiness of the public, due to the spread of literacy and democratic forms of government, to feel that it is entitled to its voice in the conduct of these large aggregations, political, capitalist or labor, or whatever they may be; third, the keen competition for public favor due to modern methods of "selling."

An example of the first tendency—that is, the tendency toward an increased public interest in industrial activity, because of the increasing social importance of industrial aggregations—may be found in an article "The Critic and the Law" by Richard Washburn Child, published in the *Atlantic Monthly* for May, 1906.

Mr. Child discusses in that article the right of the critic to say uncomplimentary things about matters of public interest. He points out the legal basis for the right to criticize plays and novels. Then he adds, "A vastly more important and interesting theory, and one which must arise from the present state and tendency of industrial conditions, is whether the acts of men in commercial activity may ever become so prominent and so far reaching in their effect that they compel a universal public interest and that public comment is impliedly invited by reason of their conspicuous and semi-public nature. It may be said that at no time have private industries become of such startling interest to the community at large as at present in the United States." How far present-day tendencies have borne out Mr. Child's expectation of a growing sand accepted public interest in important industrial enterprises, the reader can judge for himself.

With regard to the second tendency—the increased readiness of the public to expect information about and to be heard on matters of political and social interest—Ray Stannard Baker's description of the American journalist at the Peace Conference of Versailles gives an excellent picture. Mr. Baker tells what a shock American newspaper men gave Old World diplomats because at the Paris conference they "had come, not begging, but demanding." "They sat at every doorway," says Mr. Baker. "They looked over every shoulder. They wanted every resolution and report and wanted it immediately. I shall never forget the delegation of American newspaper men, led by John Nevlin, I saw come striding through that Holy of Holies, the French Foreign Office, demanding that they be admitted to the first general session of the Peace Conference. They horrified the upholders of the old methods, they desperately offended the ancient conventions, they were as rough and direct as democracy itself."

And I shall never forget the same feeling brought home to me, when Herbert Bayard Swope of the *New York World*, in the press room at the Crillon Hotel in Paris, led the discussion of the newspaper representatives who forced the conference to regard public opinion and admit newspaper men, and give out communiqués daily.

That the pressure of the public for admittance to the mysteries of foreign affairs is being felt by the nations of the world may be seen from the following dispatch published in the *New York Herald* under the date line of the *New York Herald* Bureau, Paris, January 17, 1922: "The success of Lord Riddell in getting publicity for British opinion during the Washington conference, while the French viewpoint was not stressed, may result in the appointment by the Poincaré Government of a real propaganda agent to meet the foreign newspaper men. The Éclair today calls on the new premier to 'find his own Lord Riddell in the French diplomatic and parliamentary world, who can give the world the French interpretation.'" Walter Lippmann of the *New York World* in his volume *Public Opinion* declares that the "significant revolution of modern times is not industrial or economic or political, but the revolution which is taking place in the art of creating consent among the governed." He goes on: "Within the life of the new generation now in control of affairs, persuasion has become a self-conscious art and a regular organ of popular government. None of us begins to understand the consequences, but it is no daring prophecy to say that the knowledge of how to create consent will alter every political premise. Under the impact of propaganda, not necessarily in the sinister meaning of the world alone, the only constants of our thinking have become variables. It is no longer possible, for example, to believe in the cardinal dogma of democracy, that the knowledge needed for the management of human affairs comes up spontaneously from the human heart. Where we act on that theory we expose ourselves to self-deception and to forms of persuasion that we cannot verify. It has been demonstrated that we cannot rely upon intuition, conscience, or the accidents of casual opinion if we are to deal with the world beyond our reach."[1]

In domestic affairs the importance of opinion not only in political decisions but in the daily industrial life of the nation may be seen from numerous incidents. In the *New York Times* of Friday, May 20, 1922, I find almost a column article with the heading "Hoover Prescribes Publicity for Coal." Among the improvements in the coal industry generally, which Mr. Hoover, according to the dispatch, anticipates from widespread, accurate and informative publicity about the industry itself, are the stimulation of industrial consumers to more regular demands, the ability to forecast more reliably the volume of demand, the ability of the consumer to "form some judgment as to the prices he should pay for coal," and the tendency to hold down over-expansion in the industry by publication of the ratio of production to capacity. Mr. Hoover concludes that really informative publicity "would protect the great majority of operators from the criticism that can only be properly leveled at the minority." Not so many years ago neither the majority nor the minority in the coal industry would have concerned itself about public criticism of the industry.

From coal to jewelry seems rather a long step, and yet in *The Jeweler's Circular*, a trade magazine, I find much comment upon the National Jewelers' Publicity Association. This association began with the simple commercial ambition of acquainting the public with "the value of jewelry merchandise for gift purposes."; now it finds itself engaged in eliminating from the public mind in general, and from the minds of legislators in particular, the impression that "the jewelry

---

1. Walter Lippman, *Public Opinion*, page 248.

business is absolutely useless and that any money spent in a jewelry store is thrown away."

Not so long ago it would scarcely have occurred to anyone in the jewelry industry that there was any importance to be attached to the opinion of the public on the essential or non-essential character of the jewelry industry. Today, on the other hand, jewelers find it a profitable investment to bring before the people the fact that table silver is an essential in modern life, and that without watches "the business and industries of the nation would be a sad chaos." With all the other competing interests in the world today, the question as to whether the public considers the business of manufacturing and selling jewelry essential or non-essential is a matter of the first importance to the industry.

The best examples, of course, of the increasing importance of public opinion to industries which until recently scarcely concerned themselves with the existence or non-existence of a public opinion about them, are those industries which are charged with a public interest. In a long article about the attitude of the public towards the railroads, the *Railway Age* reaches the conclusion that the most important problem which American railroads must solve is "the problem of selling themselves to the public." Some public utilities maintain public relations departments, whose function it is to interpret the organizations to the public, as much as to interpret the public to them. The significant thing, however, is not the accepted importance of public opinion in this or the other individual industry, but the fact that public opinion is becoming cumulatively more and more articulate and therefore more important to industrial life as a whole.

The New York Central Railroad, for example, maintains a Public Relations Department under Pitt Hand, whose function it is to make it clear to the public that the railroad is functioning efficiently to serve the public in every possible way. This department studies the public and tries to discover where the railroad's service can be mended or improved, or when wrong or harmful impressions upon the public mind may be corrected.

This Public Relations Department finds it profitable not only to bring to the attention of the public the salient facts about its trains, its timetables, and its actual traveling facilities, but also to build up a broadly cooperative spirit that is indirectly of great value to itself and of benefit to the public. It cooperates, for example, with such movements as the Welcome Stranger Committee of New York City in distributing literature to travelers to assist them when they reach the city. It cooperates with conventions, to the extent of arranging special travel facilities. Such aids as it affords to the directors of children's camps at the Grand Central Station are especially conspicuous for their dramatic effect on the general public.

Even a service which is in a large measure non-competitive must continually "sell" itself to the public, as evidenced by the strenuous efforts of the New York subways and elevated lines to keep themselves constantly before the people in the most favorable possible aspect. The subways strive in this regard to create a feeling of submissiveness toward inconveniences which are more or less unavoidable, and they strive likewise to fulfill such constructive programs as that of extending traffic on less frequented lines.

Let us analyze, for example, the activities of the health departments of such large cities as New York. Of recent years, Health

Commissioner Royal S. Copeland and his statements have formed a fairly regular part of the day's news. Publicity is, in fact, one of the major functions of the Health Department, inasmuch as its constructive work depends to a considerable extent upon the public education it provides in combating evils and in building up a spirit of individual and group cooperation in all health matters. When the Health Department recognizes that such diseases as cancer, tuberculosis and those following malnutrition are due generally to ignorance or neglect and that amelioration or prevention will be the result of knowledge, it is the next logical step for this department to devote strenuous efforts to its public relations campaign. The department accordingly does exactly this.

Even governments today act upon the principle that it is not sufficient to govern their own citizens well and to assure the people that they are acting whole-heartedly in their behalf. They understand that the public opinion of the entire world is important to their welfare. Thus Lithuania, already noted, while it had the unbounded love and support of its own people, was nevertheless in danger of extinction because it was unknown outside of the immediate boundaries of those nations which had a personal interest in it. Lithuania was wanted by Poland; it was wanted by Russia. It was ignored by other nations. Therefore, through the aid of a public relations expert, Lithuania issued pamphlets, it paraded, it figured in pictures and motion pictures and developed a favorable sentiment throughout the world that in the end gave Lithuania its freedom.

In industry and business, of course, there is another consideration of first-rate importance, besides the danger of interference by the public in the conduct of the industry—the increasing intensity of competition. Business and sales are no longer to be had, if ever they were to be had for the asking. It must be clear to anyone who has looked through the mass of advertising in street cars, subways, newspapers and magazines, and the other avenues of approach to the public, that products and services press hard upon one another in the effort to focus public attention on their offerings and to induce favorable action.

The keen competition in the selling of products for public favor makes it imperative that the seller consider other things than merely his product in trying to build up a favorable public reaction. He must either himself appraise the public mind and his relation to it or he must engage the services of an expert who can aid him to do this. He may today consider, for instance, in his sales campaign, not only the quality of his soap but the working conditions, the hours of labor, even the living conditions of the men who make it.

The public relations counsel must advise him on these factors as well as on the presentation to the public most interested in them.

In this state of affairs it is not at all surprising that industrial leaders should give the closest attention to public relations in both the broadest and the most practical concept of the term.

Large industrial groups, in their associations, have assigned a definite place to public relations bureaus.

The Trade Association Executives in New York, an association of individual executives of state, territorial or national trade associations, such as the Allied Wall Paper Industry, the American Hardware Manufacturers' Association, the American Protective Tariff League, the Atlantic Coast Shipbuilders' Association, the National Association of Credit Men, the Silk Association of America and some seventy-four others, includes among its associations' functions such activities as the following: cooperative advertising; adjustments and collections; cost accounting; a credit bureau; distribution and new markets; educational, standardization and research work; exhibits; a foreign trade bureau; house organs; general publicity; an industrial bureau; legislative work; legal aid; market reports; statistics; a traffic department; Washington representation; arbitration. It is noteworthy that forty of these associations have incorporated public relations with general publicity as a definite part of their program in furthering the interest of their organizations.

The American Telephone and Telegraph Company devotes effort to studying its public relations problems, not only to increase its volume of business, but also to create a cooperative spirit between itself and the public. The work of the telephone company's operators, statistics, calls, lineage, installations are given to the public in various forms. During the war and for a period afterwards its main problem was that of satisfying the public that its service was necessarily below standard because of the peculiar national conditions. The public, in response to the efforts of the company, which were analogous to a gracious personal apology, accepted more or less irksome conditions as a matter of course. Had the company not cared about the public, the public would undoubtedly have been unpleasantly insistent upon a maintenance of the pre-war standards of service.

Americans were once wont to jest about the dependence of France and Switzerland upon the tourist trade. Today we see American cities competing, as part of their public relations programs, for conventions, fairs and conferences. The *New York Times* printed some time ago an address by the governor of Nebraska, in which he told a group of advertising men that publicity had made Nebraska prosper.

The *New York Herald* carried an editorial recently, entitled, "It Pays A State To Advertise," centering about the campaign of the state of Vermont to present itself favorably to public attention. According to the editorial, the state publishes a magazine, *The Vermonter*, an attractive publication filled with interesting illustrations and well-written text. It is devoted exclusively to revealing in detail the industrial and agricultural resources of the state and to presenting Vermont's strikingly beautiful scenic attractions for the summer visitor. Similar instances of elaborate efforts, taking the form of action or the printed word, either to obtain public attention or to obtain a favorable attitude from the public for individual industries and groups of industries, will come readily to the reader's mind.

Without attempting to take too seriously an amusing story printed in a recent issue of a New York newspaper, leaders in movements and industries of modern life will be inclined to agree with the protagonist of publicity spoken of. According to the story, a man set out to prove to another that it was not so much what a man did as the way it was heralded which insures his place in history. He cited Barbara Frietchie, Evangeline, John Smith and a half dozen others as instances to prove that they are remembered not for what they did, but because they had excellent counsel on their public relations.

"'Very good,' agreed the friend. "But show me a case where a person who has really done a big thing has been overlooked.'

"'You know Paul Revere, of course,' he said. 'But tell me the names of the two other fellows who rode that night to rouse the countryside with the news that the British were coming.'

"'Never heard of them,' was the answer.

"'There were three waiting to see the signal hung in the tower of the Old North Church,' he said. 'Every one of them was mounted and spurred just as Mr. Longfellow described Paul Revere. They all got the signal. They all rode and waked the farmers, spreading the warning. Afterward one of them was an officer in Washington's army, another became governor of one of the States. Not one in twenty thousand Americans ever heard the names of the other two, and there is hardly a person in America who does not know all about Revere.'

"Did Revere make history or did Longfellow?'"

PART II:

The Group and the Herd

CHAPTER I

WHAT CONSTITUTES PUBLIC OPINION?

THE CHARACTER AND ORIGINS OF PUBLIC OPINION, the factors that make up the individual mind and the group mind must be understood if the profession of public relations counsel is to be intelligently practiced and its functions and possibilities accurately estimated. Society must understand the fundamental character of the work he is doing, if for no other reason than its own welfare.

The public relations counsel works with that vague, little understood, indefinite material called public opinion.

Public opinion is a term describing an ill-defined, mercurial and changeable group of individual judgments. Public opinion is the aggregate result of individual opinions —now uniform, now conflicting—of the men and women who make up society or any group of society. In order to understand public opinion, one must go back to the individual who makes up the group.

The mental equipment of the average individual consists of a mass of judgments on most of the subjects which touch his daily physical or mental life. These judgments are the tools of his daily being and yet they are his judgments, not on a basis of research and logical deduction, but for the most part dogmatic expressions accepted on the authority of his parents, his teachers, his church, and of his social, his economic and other leaders.

The public relations counsel must understand the social implications of an individual's thoughts and actions. Is it, for example, purely an accident that a man belongs to one church rather than another or to any other church at all? Is it an accident that makes Boston women prefer brown eggs and New York women white eggs? What are the factors that work in favor of conversion of a man from one political party to another or from one type of food to another?

Why do certain communities resist the prohibition law—why do others abide by it? Why is it difficult to start a new party movement—or to fight cancer? Why is it difficult to fight for sex education? Why does the free trader denounce protectionism, and vice versa?

If we had to form our own judgments on every matter, we should all have to find out many things for ourselves which we now take for granted. We should not cook our food or live in houses—in fact, we should revert to primitive living.

The public relations counsel must deal with the fact that persons who have little knowledge of a subject almost invariably form definite and positive judgments upon that subject.

"If we examine the mental furniture of the average man," says William Trotter, the author of a comprehensive study of the social psychology of the individual, "we shall find it made up of a vast number of judgments of a very precise kind upon subjects of very great variety, complexity, and difficulty. He will have fairly settled views upon the origin and nature of the universe, and upon what he will probably call its meaning; he will have conclusions as to what is to happen to him at death and after, as to what is and what should be the basis of conduct. He will know how the country should be governed, and why it is going to the dogs, why this piece of legislation is good and that bad. He will have strong views upon military and naval strategy, the principles of taxation, the use of alcohol and vaccination, the treatment of influenza, the prevention of hydrophobia, upon municipal trading, the teaching of Greek, upon what is permissible in art, satisfactory in literature, and hopeful in science.

"The bulk of such opinions must necessarily be without rational basis, since many of them are concerned with problems admitted by the expert to be still unsolved, while as to the rest it is clear that the training and experience of no average man can qualify him to have any opinion upon them at all. The rational method adequately used would have told him that on the great majority of these questions there could be for him but one attitude—that of suspended judgment."[1]

The reader will recall from his own experience an almost infinite number of instances in which the amateur has been fully prepared to deliver expert advice and to give final judgment in matters upon which his ignorance is patent to everyone except himself.

In the Middle Ages, society was convinced that there were witches. People were so positive that they burned people whom they suspected of witchcraft. Today there is an equal number of people who believe just as firmly, one way or the other, about spiritualism and spirits. They do not burn mediums. But people who have made no research of the subject pass strong denunciatory judgments. Others, no better informed, consider mediums divinely inspired. Not so long ago every intelligent man knew that the world was flat.

---

1. William Trotter, *Instincts of the Herd in Peace and War*, p. 36.

Today the average man has a belief just as firm and unknowing in the mysterious force which he has heard called atomic energy.

It is axiomatic that men who know little are often intolerant of a point of view that is contrary to their own. The bitterness that has been brought about by arguments on public questions is proverbial. Lovers have been parted by bitter quarrels on theories of pacificism or militarism; and when an argument upon an abstract question engages opponents, they often desert the main line of arguments in order to abuse each other.

How often this is true can be seen from the congressional records of controversies in which the personal attack supersedes logic. In a recent fight against the proposed tariff measures, a protagonist of protection published long vindictive statements, in which he tried to confound the character and the disinterestedness of his opponents. Logically his discussion should have been based only upon the sound economic, social and political value of the bill as presented.

A hundred leading American bankers, businessmen, professional men and economists united in public disapproval of this plan. They stated their opinion that the "American" Valuation Plan, as it was called, would endanger the prosperity of the country, that it would be inimical to our foreign relations and that it would injure the welfare of every country with whom our commercial and industrial ties were at all close. This group was a broadly representative group of men and women, yet the chairman of the Ways and Means Committee accused all these people of acting upon motives of personal gain and lack of patriotism. Prejudice superseded logic.

Intolerance is almost inevitably accompanied by a natural and true inability to comprehend or make allowance for opposite points of view. The skilled scientist who may be receptive to any promising suggestion in his own field may outside of his own field be found quite unwilling to make any attempt at understanding a point of view contrary to his own. In politics, for example, his understanding of the problem may be fragmentary, yet he will enter excitedly into discussions on bonus and ship subsidy, of which he has made no study. We find here with significant uniformity what one psychologist has called "logic-proof compartments."

The logic-proof compartment has always been with us. Scientists have lost their lives through refusing to see flaws in their theories. Intelligent mothers give food to their babies that they would manifestly forbid other mothers to give their children. Especially significant is the tendency of races to maintain religious beliefs and customs long after these have lost their meaning. Dietary laws, hygienic laws, even laws based upon geographical conditions that have been changed for more than a thousand years are still maintained in the logic-proof compartment of dogmatic adherence. There is a story that certain missionaries give money to heathen at the time of conversion and that the heathen, having got their money, bathe away their conversion in sacred streams.

The characteristic of the human mind to adhere to its beliefs is excellently summarized in the volume by Mr. Trotter to which reference has been made before. "It is clear," says Mr. Trotter, "at the outset that these beliefs are invariably regarded as rational and defended as such, while, the position of one who holds contrary views is held to be obviously unreasonable.

"The religious man accuses the atheist of being shallow and irrational, and is met by a similar reply. To the Conservative the amazing thing about the Liberal is his incapacity to see reason and accept the only possible solution of public problems. Examination reveals the fact that the differences are not due to the commission of the mere mechanical fallacies of logic, since these are easily avoided, even by the politician, and since there is no reason to believe that one party in such controversies is less logical than the other. The difference is due rather to the fundamental assumptions of the antagonists being hostile, and these assumptions are derived from herd-suggestions; to the Liberal certain basal conceptions have acquired the quality of instinctive truth, have become *a priori* syntheses, because of the accumulated suggestions to which he has been exposed; and a similar explanation applies to the atheist, the Christian, and the Conservative. Each, it is important to remember, finds in consequence the rationality of his position flawless and is quite incapable of detecting in it the fallacies which are obvious to his opponent, to whom that particular series of assumptions has not been rendered acceptable by herd suggestion."[2]

Thus the public relations counsel has to consider the *a priori* judgment of any public he deals with before counseling any step that would modify those things in which the public has established belief. It is seldom effective to call names or to attempt to discredit the beliefs themselves. The counsel on public relations, after examination of the sources of established beliefs, must either discredit the old authorities or create new authorities by making articulate a mass opinion against the old belief or in favor of the new.

---

2. William Trotter, *Instincts of the Herd in Peace and War*, pp.36–37.

CHAPTER II

IS PUBLIC OPINION STUBBORN OR MALLEABLE?

THERE IS A DIVERGENCE OF OPINION as to whether the public mind is malleable or stubborn—whether it is a passive or an active element. On the one hand is the profound belief that "you can't change human nature." On the other hand is the equally firm assurance that certain well-defined institutions modify and alter public opinion.

There is a uniformity of opinion in this country upon many issues. When this uniformity accords with our own beliefs we call it an expression of the public conscience. When, however, it runs contrary to our beliefs we call it regimentation of the public mind and are inclined to ascribe it to insidious propaganda.

Uniformity is, in fact, largely natural and only partly artificial. Public opinion may be as much the producer of "insidious propaganda" as its product. Naturally enough, where broad ideas are involved, criticisms of the state of the public's mind and of its origin come most frequently from groups that are out of sympathy with the accepted point of view. They find the public unreceptive to their point of view, and justly or unjustly they attribute this to the influence of antagonistic interests upon the public mind.

These groups see the press, the lecture platform, the schools, the advertisements, the churches, the radio, the motion picture screen, the magazines daily reaching millions. They see that the preponderant point of view in most, if not all, these institutions conforms to the preponderant state of mind of the public.

They argue from the one to the other and reach their conclusions without much difficulty. They do not stop to think that agreement in point of view between the public and these institutions may often be the result of the control exercised by the public mind over these institutions.

Many outside forces, however, do go to influence public opinion. The most obvious of these forces are parental influence, the school room, the press, motion pictures, advertising, magazines, lectures, the church, the radio.

To answer the question as to the stubbornness or malleability of the public, let us analyze the press in its relation to public opinion, since the press stands preeminent among the various institutions which are commonly designated as leaders or molders of the public mind. By the press, in this instance, I mean the daily press. Americans are a newspaper reading public. They have become accustomed to look to their morning and evening papers for the news of the world and for the opinions of their leaders. And while the individual newspaper reader does not give a very considerable portion of his day to this occupation, many persons find time to read more than one newspaper every day.

It is not surprising that the man who is outside the current of prevailing public opinion should regard the daily press as a coercive force.

Discussions of the public's reaction to the press are two sided, just as are the discussions of the influence of the pulpit or other forces. Some authorities hold that the public mind is stubborn in regard to the press and that the press has little influence upon it. There are graphic instances of the stubbornness of the public point of view. A most interesting example is the reelection of Mayor Haylan of New York by an overwhelming majority in the face of the opposition of all but two of the metropolitan dailies. It is also noteworthy that in 1909, Gaynor was elected Mayor of New York with every paper except one opposing his candidacy. Likewise, Mayor Mitchel of New York was defeated for reelection in 1917, although all the New York papers except two Hearst papers and the *New York Call* supported him. In Boston, in a recent election, a man was elected as mayor who had been convicted of a penal offense, and elected in the face of the practically united opposition of all the newspapers of that city. How would such authors as Everett Dean Martin, Walter Lippmann, and Upton Sinclair explain these incidents? How, on the theory of the regimentation of the public mind by the daily press, can such thinkers explain the sharpness with which the public sometimes rejects the advocacies of a united press? These instances are not frequent; but they show that other influences beside the press enter into the making of a public opinion and that these forces must never be disregarded in the estimate of the quality and stability of a prevalent public opinion.

Francis E. Leupp, writing in the *Atlantic Monthly* for February, 1910, on "The Waning Power of the Press," remarks that Mayor Gaynor's comments shortly after his election in 1909 "led up to the conclusion that in our common sense generation nobody cares what the newspapers say." Mr. Leupp continues: "Unflattering as such a verdict may be, probably the majority of a community if polled as a jury would concur in it. The airy dismissal of some proposition as 'mere newspaper talk' is heard at every social gathering until one who is brought up to regard the press as a mighty factor in modern civilization is tempted to wonder whether it has actually lost the power it used to wield among us."

And H. L. Mencken, writing in the same magazine for March, 1914, declares that "one of the principal marks of an educated man, indeed, is the fact that he does not take his opinions from newspapers—not, at any rate, from the militant, crusading newspapers. On the contrary, his attitude toward them is almost always one of frank cynicism, with indifference as its mildest form and contempt as its commonest. He knows that they are constantly falling into false reasoning about the things within his personal knowledge—that is, within the narrow circle of his special education—and so he assumes that they make the same, or even worse, errors about other things, whether intellectual or moral. This assumption, it may be said, is quite justified by the facts."

The second point of view holds that the daily press and the other leading forces merely accept, reflect and intensify established public opinion and are, therefore, responsible for the uniformity of public reaction. A vivid statement of the point of view of the man who typifies this group is found in Everett Dean Martin's volume on *The Behavior of Crowds*. He says: "The modern man has in the printing press a wonderfully effective means for perpetuating crowd-movements and keeping great masses of people constantly under the sway of certain crowd-ideas. Every crowd-group has its magazines, press agents, and special 'literature' with which it continually harangues its members and possible converts. Many books, and especially certain works of fiction of the 'best seller' type, are clearly reading mob phenomena."[1]

There is a third group which perhaps comes nearer the truth, which holds that the press, just as other mediums of education or dissemination, brings about a very definite change in public opinion. A most graphic illustration of what such mediums can do to change opinions upon fundamental and important matters is the woman suffrage question and its victory over established points of view. The press, the pulpit, the lecture platform, the motion pictures and the other mediums for reaching the public brought about a complete popular conversion. Other examples of the change that may be brought about in public opinion in this way, by such institutions of authority, is the present attitude towards birth control and towards health education.

Naturally the press, like other institutions which present facts or opinions, is restricted, often unconsciously, sometimes consciously, by various controlling conditions. Certain people talk of the censorship enacted by the prejudices and predispositions of the public itself. Some, such as Upton Sinclair, ascribe to the advertisers a conscious and powerful control of publications. Others, like Walter Lippmann, find that an effective barrier between the public and the event exists in the powerful influence which, he says, is exerted in certain cases on the press by the so-called quality public which the newspapers' advertisers wish to reach and among whom the newspapers must circulate if the advertising is to be successful. Mr. Lippmann observes that although such a restriction may exist, much of what may be attributed to censorship in the newspaper often is actually inadequate presentation of the events it seeks to describe.

---

1. Everett Dean Martin, *The Behavior of Crowds*, p.45.

On this point he says: "It follows that in the reporting of strikes, the easiest way is to let the news be uncovered by the overt act, and to describe the event as the story of the interference with the reader's life. This is where his attention is first aroused and his interest most easily enlisted. A great deal, I think myself, of the crucial part of what looks to the worker and the reformer as deliberate misrepresentation on the part of newspapers, is the direct outcome of a practical difficulty in uncovering the news, and the emotional difficulty of making distinct facts interesting unless, as Emerson says, we can 'perceive' (them) and can 'set about translating (them) at once into parallel facts.'"[2]

In view then of the possibility of a malleable public opinion the counsel on public relations, desiring to obtain a hearing for any given cause, simply utilizes existent channels to obtain expression for the point of view he represents. How this is done will be considered later.

Because of the importance of channels of thought communication, it is vital for the public relations counsel to study carefully the relationship between public opinion and the organs that maintain it or that influence it to change. We shall look into this interaction and its effect in the next chapter.

---

2. Walter Lippmann, *Public Opinion*, p.350.

CHAPTER III

THE INTERACTION OF PUBLIC OPINION WITH THE FORCES THAT HELP TO MAKE IT

THE PUBLIC AND THE PRESS, OR for that matter, the public and any force that modifies public opinion, interact. Action and interaction are continually going on between the forces projected out to the public and the public itself. The public relations counsel must understand this fact in its broadest and most detailed implications. He must understand not only what these various forces are, but he must be able to evaluate their relative powers with fair accuracy. Let us consider again the case of a newspaper, as representative of other mediums of communications.

"We print," says the *New York Times*, "all news that's fit to print." Immediately the question arises (as Elmer Davis, the historian of the *Times* tells us that it did when the motto was first adopted) what news is fit to print? By what standard is the editorial decision reached which includes one kind of news and excludes another kind? The *Times* itself has not been, in its long and conspicuously successful career, entirely free from difficulties on this point.

Thus in "The History of the *New York Times*," Mr. Davis feels the need for justifying the extent to which that paper featured Theodore Tilton's action against the Rev. Henry Ward Beecher for alienation of Mrs. Tilton's affections and his conduct with her. Mr. Davis says (pages 124–25): "No doubt a good many readers of the *Times* thought the paper was giving an undue amount of space to this chronicle of sin and suffering. Those complaints come often enough even in these days from readers who appreciate the paper's general reluctance to display news of this sort, and wonder why a good general rule should occasionally be violated. But there was a reason in the Beecher case, as there has usually been a reason in similar affairs since. Dr. Beecher was one of the most prominent clergymen in the country; there was a natural curiosity as to whether he was practicing what he preached. One of the counsels at the trial declared that 'all Christendom was hanging on its outcome.' Full reporting of its course was not a mere pandering to vulgar curiosity, but a recognition of the value of the case as news."

The simple fact that such a slogan can exist and be accepted is for our purpose an important point. Somewhere there must be a standard to which the editors of the *Times* can conform, as well as a larger clientele of constant readers to whom that standard is satisfactory. "Fit" must be defined by the editors of the *Times* in a way which meets with the approval of enough persons to enable the paper to maintain its reading public. As soon, however, as the definition is attempted, difficulties arise.

Professor W. G. Bleyer, in an article in his book on journalism, first stresses the importance of completeness in the news columns of a paper, then goes on to say that "the only important limitations to completeness are those imposed by the commonly accepted ideas of decency embodied in the words, 'All the news that's fit to print' and by the rights of privacy. Carefully edited newspapers discriminate between what the public is entitled to know and what an individual has a right to keep private."

On the other hand, when Professor Bleyer attempts to define what news is fit to print and what the public is entitled to know, he discusses generalizations capable of wide and frequently inconsistent interpretation. "News," says he, "is anything timely which is significant to newspaper readers in their relations to the community, the state and the nation."

Who is to determine what is significant and what is not? Who is to decide which of the individual's relations to the community are safeguarded by his right of privacy and which are not? Such a definition tells us nothing more definite than does the slogan which it attempts to define. We must look further for a standard by which these definitions are applied. There must be a consensus of public opinion on which the newspaper falls back for its standards.

The truth is that while it appears to be forming the public opinion on fundamental matters, the press is often conforming to it.

It is the office of the public relations counsel to determine the interaction between the public, and the press and the other mediums affecting public opinion. It is as important to conform to the standards of the organ which projects ideas as it is to present to this organ such ideas as will conform to the fundamental understanding and appreciation of the public to which they are ultimately to appeal. There is as much truth in the proposition that the public leads institutions as in the contrary proposition that the institutions lead the public.

As an illustration of the manner in which newspapers are inclined to accept the judgments of their readers in presenting material to them, we have this anecdote which Rollo Ogden tells in the *Atlantic Monthly* for July, 1906, about a letter which Wendell Phillips wished to have published in a Boston paper.

"The editor read it over, and said, 'Mr. Phillips, that is a very good and interesting letter, and I shall be glad to publish it; but I wish you would consent to strike out the last paragraph.'

"Why,' said Phillips, 'that paragraph is the precise thing for which I wrote the whole letter. Without that it would be pointless.'

"Oh, I see that,' replied the editor; 'and what you say is perfectly true! I fully agree with it all myself. Yet it is one of those things which will not do to say publicly. However, if you insist upon it, I will publish it as it stands.'

"It was published the next morning, and along with it a short editorial reference to it, saying that a letter from Mr. Phillips would be found in another column, and that it was extraordinary that so keen a mind as his should have fallen into the palpable absurdity contained in the last paragraph."

Recognition of this fact comes from a number of different sources. H. L. Mencken recognizes that the public runs the press as much as the press runs the public. "The primary aim of all of them," says Mr. Mencken, "not less when they play the secular Iokanaan than when they play the mere newsmonger, was to please the crowd, and to give a good show; and the way they set about giving that good show was by first selecting a deserving victim, and then putting him magnificently to the torture.

"This was their method when they were performing for their own profit only, when their one motive was to make the public read their paper; but it was still their motive when they were battling bravely and unselfishly for the public good, and so discharging the highest duty of their profession."[1]

---

1. H. L. Mencken, *Atlantic Monthly*, March, 1914.

There are interesting, if somewhat obscure examples of the complementary working of various forces. In the field of the motion pictures, for example, the producers, the actors, and the press, in their support, have continually waged a battle against censorship. Undoubtedly censorship of the motion pictures is in its practical workings an economic and artistic handicap. Censorship, however, will continue in spite of the producers as long as there is a willingness on the part of the public to accept this censorship. The public, on the whole, has refused to join the fight against censorship, because there is a more or less articulate belief that children, if not women, should be protected from seeing shocking sights, such as murders visibly enacted, the taking of drugs, immoralities and other acts which might offend or suggest harmful imitation.

Damaged Goods, before its presentation to America in 1913, was analyzed by the public relations counsel, who helped to produce the play. He recognized that unless that part of the public sentiment which believed in education and truth could be lifted from that part of public opinion which condemned the mentioning of sex matters, *Damaged Goods* would fail. The producers, therefore, did not try to educate the public by presenting this play as such, but allowed group leaders and groups interested in education to come to the support of Brieux's drama and, in a sense, to sponsor the production.

Proof that the public and the institutions that make public opinion interact is shown in instances in which books were stifled because of popular disapproval at one time and then brought forward by popular demand at a later time when public opinion had altered. Religious and very early scientific works are among such books.

A more recent instance is the announcement made by *Judge*, a weekly magazine, that it would support the fight for light wine and beer. Judge took this stand because it believed in the principle of personal freedom and also because it deemed that public sentiment was in favor of light wine and beer as a substitute for absolute prohibition. *Judge* believed its stand would please its readers.

Presumably writing of newspaper morality, Mr. Mencken, in his article just quoted, finds at the end of it that he has "written of popular morality very copiously, and of newspaper morality very little.

"But," says Mr. Mencken, "as I have said before, the one is the other. The newspaper must adapt its pleading to its clients' moral limitation just as the trial lawyer also must adapt his pleading to the jury's limitations. Neither may like the job, but both must face it to gain the larger end."

Writing on the other hand from the point of view of the man who feels that the public taste requires no justification, Ralph Pulitzer nevertheless agrees with Mr. Mencken that the opinion of the press is set by the public; and he justifies "muckraking"[2] by finding it neither "extraordinary nor culpable that people and press should be more interested in the polemical than in the platitudinous; in blame than in painting the lily; in attack than in sending laudatory coals to Newcastle."[2]

Even Mr. Leupp concludes that "whatever we may say of the modern press on its less commendable side, we are bound to admit that newspapers, like governments, fairly reflect the people they serve. Charles Dudley Warner once went so far as to say that no matter how objectionable the character of a paper may be, it is always

2. *Atlantic Monthly*, March, 1914.

a trifle better than the patrons on whom it relies for its support."[3]

Similarly, from an unusually wide experience on a paper as highly considered, perhaps, as any in America, Rollo Ogden claims this give and take between the public and the press is vital to a just conception of American journalism.

"The editor does not nonchalantly project his thoughts into the void. He listens for the echo of his words. His reaction to his supporters is not unlike Gladstone's definition of the intimate connection between the orator and his audience. As the speaker gets from his hearers in mist what he gives back in shower, so the newspaper receives from the public as well as it gives back to it. Too often it gets as dust what it gives back as mud; but that does not alter the relations. Action and reaction are all the while going on between the press and its patrons.

Hence it follows that the responsibility for the more crying evils of journalism must be divided."[4]

This same interaction goes on in connection with all the other forces that mold public opinion. The preacher upholds the ideals of society. He leads his flock wither they indicate a willingness to be led. Ibsen creates a revolution when society is ripe for it. The public responds to finer music and better motion pictures and demands improvements. "Give the people what they want" is only half sound. What they want and what they get are fused by some mysterious alchemy. The press, the lecturer, the screen and the public lead and are led by each other.

---

3. Frances E. Leupp, "The Waning Power of the Press," *Atlantic Monthly*, July, 1910.

4. Rollo Ogden, "Some Aspects of Journalism," *Atlantic Monthly*, July, 1906.

CHAPTER IV

THE POWER OF INTERACTING FORCES THAT GO TO MAKE UP PUBLIC OPINION

THE INFLUENCE OF ANY FORCE WHICH attempts to modify public opinion depends upon the success with which it is able to enlist established points of view. A middle ground exists between the hypothesis that the public is stubborn and the hypothesis that it is malleable. To a large degree the press, the schools, the churches, motion pictures, advertising, the lecture platform and radio all conform to the demands of the public. But to an equally large degree the public responds to the influence of these very same mediums of communication.

Some analysts believe that the public has no opinions except those which various institutions provide ready made for it. From Mr. Mencken and others it would almost seem to follow that newspapers and other mediums have no standards except those which the public provides, and that therefore they are substantially without influence upon the public mind. The truth of the matter, as I have pointed out, lies somewhere between these two extreme positions.

In other words, the public relations counsel who thinks clearly on the problem of public opinion and public relations will credit the two factors of public opinion respectively with their influence and effectiveness in mutual interaction. Ray Stannard Baker says that "while there was a gesture of unconcern, of don't care what they say, on the part of the leaders (of the Versailles conference), no aspect of the conference in reality worried them more than the news, opinions, guesses that went out by scores of thousands of words every night, and the reactions which came back so promptly from them. The problems of publicity consumed an astonishing amount of time, anxiety and discussion among the leaders of the conference. It influenced the entire procedure, it was partly instrumental in driving the four heads of States finally into small secret conferences. The full achievement of publicity on one occasion—Wilson's Italian note—nearly broke up the conference and overturned a government. The bare threat of it, upon other occasions, changed the course of the discussion. Nothing concerned the conference more than what democracy was going to do with diplomacy."[1]

For like causes we find great industries—motion pictures being one and organized baseball another—appointing as directors of their activities men prominent in public life, doing this to assure the public of the honest and social-minded conduct of their members. The Franklin Roosevelts are in this class, the Will Hayes and the Landises.

A striking example of this interaction is illustrated in what occurred at the Hague Conference a few years ago. The effect of the Hague Conference's conduct upon the public was such that officials were forced to open the Conference doors to the representatives of newspapers. On June 16th, 1922, a note came from The Hague by the Associated Press that Foreign Minister Van Karnebeek of Holland capitulated to the world's desire to be informed of what was going on

---

1. "Publicity at Paris," *New York Times*, April 2, 1922.

by ad correspondents. Early announcement that "the press cannot be admitted" was, according to the report, followed by anxious emissaries begging the journalists to have patience. Editorials printed in Holland pointed out that the best way to insure public cooperation was to take the public into its confidence. Minister van Karnebeek, who had been at Washington, was thoroughly awake to the invaluable service the press of the world rendered there. One editorial here pointed out that public statements "were used by the diplomats themselves as a happy means of testing popular opinion upon the various projects offered in council. How many 'trial balloons' were sent up in this fashion, nobody can recall. Nevertheless each delegation maintained clipping bureaus, which were brought up to date every morning and which gave the delegates accurate information as to the state of mind at home. Thus it came about that world opinion was ready and anxious to receive the finished work of the conference and that it was prompt to bring individual recalcitrant groups into line."

Let me quote from the *New York Evening Post* of July, 1922, as to the important interaction of these forces: "The importance of the press in guiding public opinion and the cooperation between the members of the press and the men who express public opinion in action, which has grown up since the Peace Conference at Paris, were stressed by Lionel Curtis, who arrived on the Adriatic yesterday to attend the Institute of Politics, which opens on July 27 at Williamstown. 'Perhaps for the first time in history,' he said, 'the men whose business it is to make public opinion were collected for some months under the same roof with the officials whose task in life is the actual conduct of foreign affairs. In the long run, foreign policy is determined by public opinion. It was impossible in Paris not to be impressed by the immense advantage of bringing into close contact the writers who, through the press, are making public opinion, and the men who have to express their opinion in actual policy.'"

Harvard University, likewise, appreciating the power of public opinion over its own activities, has recently appointed a counsel on public relations to make its aims clear to the public.

The institutions which make public opinion conform to the demands of the public. The public responds to an equally large degree to these institutions. Such fights as that made by *Collier's Weekly* for pure food control show this.

The Safety First movement, by its use of every form of appeal, from poster to circular, from lecture to law enforcement, from motion pictures to "safety weeks," is bringing about a gradual change in the attitude of a safety-deserving public towards the taking of unnecessary risks.

The Rockefeller Foundation, confronted with the serious problem of the hookworm in the South and in other localities, has brought about a change in the habits of large sections of rural populations by analysis, investigation, applied medical principles, and public education.

The molder of public opinion must enlist the established point of view. This is true of the press as well as of other forces. Mr. Mencken mixes cynicism and truth when he declares that the chief difficulty confronting a newspaper which tries to carry out independent and thoughtful policies "does not lie in the direction of the board of directors, but in the direction of the public which buys the paper."[2]

The *New York Tribune*, as an example of editorial bravery, points

---

2. H.L. Mencken, "On Journalism," *The Nation*, April 26, 1922.

out in an advertisement published May 23, 1922, that though "news knows no order in the making" and though "a newspaper must carry the news, both pleasant and unpleasant," nevertheless, it is the duty of any newspaper to realize that there is a possibility of selective action, and that "in times of stress and bleak despair a newspaper has a hard and fast duty to perform in keeping up the morale of the community." Indeed, the instances are frequent and accessible to the recollection of any reader in which newspapers have consciously maintained a point of view toward which the public is either hostile or cold.

Occasionally, of course, even the established point of view is alterable. The two *Baltimore Suns* do brave their public and have been braving their public for some time, not entirely without success. As severe a critic as Oswald Garrison Villard points out that though modern Baltimore is a difficult city to serve, yet the two *Suns* have courageously and consistently stood for the policies of their editors and have refused to yield to pressure from any source. To the public relations counsel this is a striking illustration of the give and take between the public and the institutions which attempt to mold public opinion. The two interact upon each other, so that it is sometimes difficult to tell which is one and which is the other.

The World and the *Evening World of New York* pride themselves upon the following campaigns which are listed in *The World Almanac* of 1922. They illustrate this interaction.

"*Conference on Limitation of Armament Grew From 'World's' Plea*
"Bearing in mind in 1921 the injunction of its founder, Joseph Pulitzer, to fight always for progress and reform, and having led the campaign for disarmament in advance

of any other demand therefore, the *World* covered the Washington Conference on Limitation of Armament in a comprehensive way . . .

"*Measures Advocated by 'World' Made Law*
"During the 1921 session of the New York Legislature many measures advocated by the *World* were enacted. One of the paper's chief achievements was the passage of a resolution broadening the power of the Lockwood Housing Committee, enabling it to inquire into high finance as related to the building trades situation.

"The *World* was instrumental in obtaining the Anti-Theater Ticket Spectacular Law. It also brought about a change in bills to abolish the Daylight-Saving Law so that municipalities might enact their own daylight-saving ordinances. It was successful in its campaign against the search-and-seizure and other drastic features of the State Prohibition Enforcement Law.

"*The 'World' Told Facts about Ku Klux Klan*
"The *World* on September 6 commenced the publication of a series of articles telling the truth about the Ku Klux Klan. Twenty-six newspapers, in widely separated sections of the United States, joined the *World* in the publication; some had been invited to participate, others requested the *World* to let them use the articles. All these newspapers realized that the only motive of the *World's* publication was public service. It was their desire to share in this service,

and the *World* is proud that they asked only assurance of its traditional accuracy and fairness before they saw their way clear to cooperation.

"The *World* is proud that the completed record shows no evidence either that it was terrified by threats or was goaded by abuse into departures from its object of presenting the facts honestly and without exaggeration.

"*Changes in Motor Vehicle Laws*
"As a result of a crusade to lessen automobile fatalities in New York City and State, the *World* won victory when changes in the motor vehicle laws were made. The paper printed exclusive stories giving the motor and license numbers of cars stolen daily in this city, and started a campaign against outlaw taxicabs and financially irresponsible drivers and owners.

"*'Evening World's' Achievements*
"The *Evening World* continued its campaign against the coal monopoly and the high coal prices charged in New York City—a state of affairs that has been constantly and vigorously exposed in *Evening World* columns. After consultation with leading Senators in Washington, several bills were introduced in Congress to alleviate the conditions."

I am letting the *World* speak for itself merely as an example of what many splendid newspapers have accomplished as leaders in public movements. The *New York Evening Post* is another example, it having long led popular demand for vocational guidance and control.

The public relations counsel cannot base his work merely upon the acceptance of the principle that the public and its authorities interact. He must go deeper than that and discover why it is that a public opinion exists independently of church, school, press, lecture platform and motion picture screen—how far this public opinion affects these institutions and how far these institutions affect public opinion. He must discover what the stimuli are to which public opinion responds most readily.

Study of the mirrors of the public mind—the press, the motion pictures, the lecture platform and the others—reveal to him what their standards are and those of the groups they reach. This is not enough, however. To his understanding of what he actually can measure he must add a thorough knowledge of the principles which govern individual and group action. A fundamental study of group and individual psychology is required before the public relations counsel can determine how readily individuals or groups will accept modifications of viewpoints or policies, which they have already imposed upon their respective mediums.

No idea or opinion is an isolated factor. It is surrounded and influenced by precedent, authority, habit and all the other human motivations.

For a lucid conception of the functions, power and social utility of the public relations counsel it is vitally important to have a clear grasp of the fundamentals with which he must work.

Emergence of the
Public Relations Counsel:
Principles and Recollections
(1971)

PUBLIC RELATIONS, A RELATIVELY NEW PROFESSION, and its practitioner, the professional counsel on public relations, serve a constructive function in our complex, free society. This profession deals with a unit's relations with the publics on which it depends. The counsel on public relations analyzes the adjustments or maladjustments between the unit and the publics on which it depends for meeting its objectives. He advises the unit on attitudes and actions necessary to meet objectives. He supplies to the public information about the unit for its consideration and action. The goals of public relations are to reach the highest possible interrelationship between a unit and its publics, based on adjustment, information, and persuasion.

Public relations came about because organized activity, which depends on public support, needed a societal technician to counsel it—the counsel on public relations. Public relations recognizes that the coincidence of private and public interest is basic to viability in a democratic society. New and faster means of communication and transportation furthered the growth of the profession. Social science research increased understanding of human behavior. The greater complexity of the society and the overlapping and interwoven network of communications that hold it together almost made the evolution of the new profession inevitable. All this requires that the counsel on public relations be a student of the social sciences in his capacity as a policy adviser and a technician. The public relations counsel meets the problem of bringing about better relations between a principal and his publics in a two-way process. He interprets public to principal and principal to public.

Public relations, effectively used, helps validate an underlying principle of our society—competition in the marketplace of ideas and things. In a democratic society almost every activity depends on public understanding and support. Many points of view are freely expressed, and they all compete for support. Public acceptance of new ideas in medicine, social service, politics, and business is brought about in the United States by public education, persuasion, and suggestion by effective public relations. This profession makes it possible for minority ideas to be more readily accepted by the majority. In playing its role in the marketplace of ideas, professional public relations depends on reality, not on images.

USE OF AN ENGINEERING APPROACH

In 1923 I laid down the principles and practices of this new profession in *Crystallizing Public Opinion*, the first book on the subject. Some fifteen years later in the light of my experience I refined the approach and called it the engineering of consent. The term engineering was used advisedly. In our society, with its myriads of group interests, interest groups, and media, only an engineering approach to the problems of adjustment, information, and persuasion could bring effective results.

There are several basic steps in the engineering of consent which apply to all public relations problems. The first is to define goals as specifically as possible. Unless we know where we want to go, it is unlikely we will get there. Goals must be defined in time periods as well as in attitudes of publics on which we depend. Time goals are immediate, intermediate, and long-term. What changes in attitude and action are we seeking, in whom and when? In any public relations problem there are many publics, seldom one. In the engineering of consent, determination of goals is subject to change after research about the relevant publics. Only after we know the state of public opinion through research can we be sure that our goals are realistic.

Research is the second step. Recent advances in public opinion research provide proven tools to evaluate the publics. Public opinion research tells us about the publics: demographic characteristics, their attitudes, motivations, how they behave and why, and what appeals may cause change. Research defines areas of ignorance, apathy and knowledge. The extent and intensity of research depend on the specific situation and on available resources. Any research of public opinion, no matter how minor, helps in the evaluation of the practicability of reaching the goals.

The next step in the engineering of consent is the consideration of a possible reorientation of goals. If research has shown the objective to be unrealistic, the goals must be modified in the light of research data.

The next problem is to design an organized effort to achieve the objective, including the utilization of manpower, mind power, mechanics, and money necessary to carry on an effective public relations program. In some cases, the public relations organization can be minimal. Authority at the top guides the actions and attitudes of personnel and makes them consistent with sound public relations. In other cases, such as in a hotel, where good public relations depends on successful employee-customer relations throughout the establishment, public relations may demand more complex organization to ensure that everyone carries out house policies. The standing of a large corporation may depend on its policies and actions related to all elements of the society. This in turn will demand a complex organization to deal with many groups and many communications media. Business organizations often rely on an outside counsel on public relations, comparable to the practice that prevails in legal relations. Often a public relations department within the corporation functions jointly with the outside advisory counsel.

Strategy is the next step in the engineering of consent. To what extent should our activity stress adjusting to the public and to what extent should it attempt to modify public apathy, misunderstanding, or ignorance? In what combination should available resources be used for greatest effectiveness? Is a blitzkrieg indicated? How do we best reach our publics? Our strategy will indicate our activities aimed at intensifying favorable attitudes and reversing or blanketing negative attitudes.

The last step is planning and timing actions to meet short-term, intermediate and long-term goals. Since public relations functions on a two-street, we may change certain of our attitudes and actions to adjust to our publics, and/or we may alter efforts to persuade our publics to support our cause or product. Many different informational techniques are used. Public relations practiced as a profession is an art applied to a science, in which the public interest and not pecuniary motivation is the primary consideration. The engineering of consent in this sense assumes a constructive social role. Regrettably, public relations, like other professions, can be abused and used for anti-social purposes. I have tried to make the profession socially responsible as well as economically viable.

EARLY EXPERIENCES IN PUBLIC RELATIONS

The events that led to my role in the engineering of consent stem from a background of lifelong interests in communication, in interpersonal and in intergroup relations. Editor of the *Echo*, P.S. 184 school paper in New York in 1905, then of the *Magpie* at the DeWitt Clinton High School in 1907 and 1908, I was also an editor of the *Cornell Countryman* at Cornell University. After graduation I became editor of the *Hygienic and Dietetic Gazette* and a member of the staff of the *Medical Review of Reviews* in 1913. I carried out my first important activity in public relations in support of an actor, Richard Bennett, who wanted to produce *Damaged Goods* by Eugene Brieux, a play about sex education. I followed a principle I often applied later, to make a cause of our project. We organized the Sociological Fund of the *Medical Review of Reviews*. A member paid four dollars and was entitled to a single performance of the play. Without such precautions, Anthony Comstock (a then-famous crusader for "high morals") would otherwise have raided it. Cosmo Hamilton, a leading British journalist, said the play made it strike sex o'clock in America. I became so intrigued by this problem of winning public support that I turned to that activity first in the theater, in music, and the ballet.

Klaw & Erlanger, leading theatrical producers, engaged me as publicist for Henry Miller, Ruth Chatterton, Otis Skinner, and other leading actors and playwrights. The Metropolitan Musical Bureau, which was associated with the Metropolitan Opera Company, made me a partner. I publicized Diaghileff, his Ballet Russe and Nijinsky, and I managed and publicized the great tenor Enrico Caruso and other Metropolitan Opera stars. I found time to become a contributor to the *Broadway Anthology,* a book of poetry in the style of Edgar Lee Masters.

After the United States entered World War I, I joined the United States Committee on Public Information, headed by George Creel. I served as a staff member of its Foreign Press Bureau headed by Ernest Poole, the novelist, in New York and later at the Peace Conference in Paris, publicizing the war aims and ideals of Woodrow Wilson—to make the world safe for democracy and to make World War I the war to end all wars.

The United States Committee on Public Information bolstered the morale of our citizens and of our allies and helped to break down enemy morale. Its propaganda efforts were so effective that one historian was later moved to write that words won the war. I returned to the United States in March, 1919, and recognized that I had learned much in the war that could be applied to peacetime pursuits. Outside of the theatrical and musical fields, I was ignorant of publicity activities in this country. In part this was because the media maintained a conspiracy of silence about the then crude practices of publicity men.

Many years later, I recognized that publicity people's lack of public visibility was possibly due to the unwillingness of the media to call attention to certain evil practices maintained by some newspapers. These activities included the practice of publishing what were called free "puffs" (editorial matter to which the newspaper committed itself in return for advertising) and the practice of extending editorial good will to railroads in return for free passes. The newspaper publishers association initiated a movement to stop the practice and to free the press from the influence of advertisers on editorial matter.

My ignorance of publicity work outside music and the theater included a lack of awareness of recent broad developments in the publicity field. In the late nineteenth century the reform movement in which unionists, Populists, Christian Socialists, and muckrakers had formerly participated, had then been joined by the middle classes. It aimed to eliminate abuses by big business, the "robber barons," and the trusts. Business had responded not by a change of attitudes and actions vis-à-vis the public but by meeting words with words. Newspaper men were hired by business as apologists. Press bureaus were organized to supply favorable information to the press. First taken up by the railroads, the public utilities, and the streetcar interests, these activities were soon practiced by many large businesses. Ivy L. Lee helped usher in this public-be-informed period in 1906 with a declaration of principles, outlining this new business publicity and information policy.

Those opposed to the practice called what was being done "whitewashing." The press agents and publicity men who carried on the activity were "space grabbers." *Editor & Publisher* and *Printers' Ink*, leading advertising journals of the period, both conducted vigorous campaigns against these "menaces."

Business had indeed become conscious of the public, which

it had not been in the earlier, public-be-damned period. But the methods it used were rudimentary in nature. They were carried on without regard to the basic principles of a profession, an art applied to a science, with the public interest the primary consideration.

Unaware of all this background, I opened in 1919 a firm to deal with broader problems of publicity than before the war. The War Department had already asked me to wage a publicity campaign for the reemployment of ex-servicemen. No G.I. Bill of Rights existed then. The re-absorption of veterans into the domestic economy was left to chance and to our office, augmented by field men from government departments.

In addition to the work for the government, the Lithuanian National Council had also come to us to win public support for its recognition by the United States as a free and independent state. Our offices to serve these clients, and more we felt were assuredly coming, were in a renovated private house at 19 East 48th Street in New York. Our office staff included Doris E. Fleischman, a brilliant young graduate of Barnard College whom I had known from my college days. I lured her from the *New York Tribune*, where she was an assistant editor. She became my wife three years later and has been my professional partner for almost fifty years. For forty-nine years we have lived our twenty-four-hour-a-day private and professional life together. It was the best move I ever made in my life.

Our first office staff consisted of seven co-workers and myself, with a payroll of $142.82 weekly. Fortunately for the workers, there were no deductions for withholding taxes. I was the contact man with the clients. My future wife was our writer and balance wheel of the operation; my brother-in-law, then a young lawyer returned from the war, also wrote material for us. A complement of stenographers, typists, and an office boy made up the remainder of our personnel. We called our activity publicity direction, directing the action of clients to secure publicity. But after a year we decided that our activity, to be really effective, needed the two-way street approach in which we interpreted the public to the client as well as vice versa. We called what we did counsel on public relations and practiced our vocation as a profession.

ACTIVITIES IN THE 1920s

During the first ten years, 1919–1929, many clients retained us. I accepted the influx as normal procedure. Retrospectively, I am baffled as to how it came about that so many outstanding American organizations sought our advice. Victor Hugo's aphorism that happy is the idea whose time has come may have been the reason. There was a growing need in New York for a constructive activity that interpreted the public interest to business, advised it on policies and programs needed to maintain public support, and in turn interpreted the business to the public.

We decided at the start to put our services on a parity with other professional services such as those of attorneys and other consultants. An early client, Lucius Boomer, who headed the Waldorf-Astoria Hotel, set the pattern for our fees in two Latin words: *quantum meruit*, what the matter is worth. Our practice was to exchange letters of agreement with clients. Our normal yearly fee was between $12,000 and $15,000, payable quarterly or monthly in advance.

In the 1920s we published an occasional four-page 8.5 x 11 leaflet, *Contact*, which my wife initiated and edited. It contained quotations relevant to our work and defined the scope and function of public relations. Group leaders and opinion molders were sent *Contact*. We made no direct effort to find clients. Until some ten years later, in the early 1930's, we received little public mention in the media. But whatever the reason—word of mouth, recommendation or casual contact—our roster of clients grew rapidly. We moved to larger, more attractive quarters in a new building at the corner of 46th Street and Fifth Avenue in 1921. To name all our clients in that first decade would be boring and unnecessary, but I should like to name a few.

Procter and Gamble, leading American manufacturers of soap and vegetable fats, retained us for counsel on public relations early in this period, and we worked together on diversified projects for over thirty years in close consultation with management. Soap sculpture became a national outlet for children's creative instincts and helped develop a generation that enjoyed cleanliness. We publicized cleanliness. We worked to make guaranteed employment more acceptable to American industry. We made social science studies of folkways and mores of communities where new plants were to be located, to ensure that acceptable patterns for employment were followed. We laid out plans for company participation in community activities. We urged the company to employ Blacks. We helped set up within the company a department of public relations, an example other companies soon followed.

The National Association for the Advancement of Colored People engaged us in connection with the first annual convention of the NAACP ever held in the South, in Atlanta, Georgia in 1920. That conference held below the Mason-Dixon line strengthened the determination of liberals of all races to fight for the world Wilson had envisioned in his ideas about making the world safe for democracy. Jim Crowism and horrible lynchings were a blot on the country. Compared to that day, things have not improved much.

In addition to work for industry and the NAACP, we engaged in counseling politicians. Alice Roosevelt Longworth had characterized Calvin Coolidge, then President of the United States, as "weaned on a pickle." His adherents engaged us to counteract the effect. We arranged a breakfast at the White House with the President to humanize his reputation. Actors and actresses, including Al Jolson, the Dolly Sisters, and others were present at this unprecedented feast, widely reported in front-page stories throughout the country. It helped to mellow the President's reputation.

We also helped Cheney Brothers, an old distinguished New England silk manufacturer, to establish their style leadership. In order to achieve that, we initiated activities to stress art in industry, a new concept then. The Luxembourg Museum in Paris held an exhibition of Cheney silks. Beauty was less than an afterthought in the mass production society of the United States of that day. The impact of "art in industry" was lasting; it changed women's wear and the decorative arts for the better. In a related experience, Secretary of Commerce Herbert Hoover appointed me Associate Commissioner to the 1925 Paris Exposition of Decorative Arts. It provided me with broader understanding of problems affecting the decorative arts industries.

The leading makers of men's clothes, Hart, Schaffner & Marx, sought our counsel to lessen risks in launching new men's fashions. The principle of group leadership dominates men's fashions, as it does women's. We cooperated with style leaders in London and on the campuses of far west universities in order to coordinate fashions of our clients with emerging tastes. Our activity for Sydney Blumenthal, velvet manufacturers, was aimed at swathing American women in velvet; and for the luggage manufacturers we attempted to increase the use of luggage. We popularized gelatine as a dessert and tried to find new uses for it. The Mellon Institute research attested to gelatine's effectiveness in improving the digestibility of milk, and we promoted gelatine as an additive to milk in school luncheon programs.

We introduced public relations practices and policies to book publishing for publisher Horace Liveright. Publishers thought of books as something to be published rather than to be sold. After our activities, book publishers took a cue from Liveright, and books soon occupied a more dynamic place in the society. *Publishers Weekly* in 1920 published my article on these new methods. Liveright's pioneering was evidenced when he published my *Crystallizing Public Opinion* in 1923.

For *Good Housekeeping* we built public support for one of the first Congressional Bills for prenatal maternal care—the Shepherd-Towner Act. We advised *Cosmopolitan* on many aspects of their public relations.

We also played a part in the introduction of new medical techniques. Madame Curie had isolated radium in Europe, and Carnotite ore containing it had been found in Colorado. The United States Radium Corporation retained us in order to gain acceptance of radium in therapy for cancer and for use in luminous gauges. In an unforgettable trip to Buffalo on the Empire State Express, I brought a gram of radium valued at $70,000; it was intended for cancer therapy at a state hospital. Scientists knew comparatively little about this rare element; fortunately the company knew enough to package the valuable but dangerous cargo in a lead container. Other hospitals followed the example of radium treatment for cancer.

George Washington Hill, a manic, boisterous, authoritarian salesman, president of the American Tobacco Company, was an exciting client for many years. Lucky Strikes were his dominating theme. Cigarettes had not yet been proven carcinogenic. Opera stars endorsed Luckies as "kind to your throat" in huge newspaper advertisements. "Reach for a Lucky, instead of a sweet" and other slogans swept the country. Lucky Strikes became the number one cigarette. Mr. Hill wanted more women to smoke Lucky Strikes; research showed that sales to them were down because the green-packaged cigarettes clashed with their costumes. "Change the color of the package," I suggested. Mr. Hill was outraged. I then suggested we try to make green the dominant color of women's fashions. "What will it cost?" he asked. For want of a better figure, I said, "$25,000." He quickly rejoindered, "Spend it." For a year we worked with the New York Infirmary for Women and Mrs. Frank A. Vanderlip, its president, to hold a Green Ball, with tableaux of socialites dressed in green based on the paintings of the Malmaison masters in the Luxembourg Museum in Paris. We worked with manufacturers of accessories for dresses and textiles to ensure that gloves, stockings, shoes, and other accessories would also be green. *Harper's Bazaar* and *Vogue* featured green covers of fashions on the date of the Green Ball. Green became fashion's color.

Another experience with fashion involved Maison Worth of the Parisian haute couture, which prided itself on dressing queens and princesses of the remaining European monarchies. They wanted to expand their markets to the United States and engaged us to help them.

Makers of food products familiar to the American palate became our clients. We staged an art show of palette oils and palate oils for Best Foods Company, makers of salad oils, at a well known New York art gallery. Favorite salad recipes of well known people and oil paintings of salads by French masters were presented in juxtaposition. Salad oil received public visibility and good will.

We counseled Beech-Nut Packing, famous for bacon and ginger ale, on many problems ranging from top-level company policy to counteracting false rumors. Sales of Beech-Nut bacon received impetus from a survey of physicians who urged Americans, as a health measure, to eat heavier breakfasts. To many this meant bacon and eggs.

In 1925 we opened the first American public relations office in Europe, in the city of Vienna. Georg Schicht, leading maker of soaps and margarine in Czechoslovakia, cabled me to survey attitudes of the people of central Europe toward margarine and butter, which we did. Schicht explained later that a standing order with a bookseller in London had brought him a copy of *Crystallizing Public Opinion*. Schicht's adoption of public relations brought it to central Europe, for the firm was a leader then. Public relations still thrives there today.

In 1928 William Paley of Columbia Broadcasting, then owner of only one radio station, called on us for advice. Young Paley, tired of Philadelphia and disenchanted with his father's cigar business, had received as a gift from his father WCBS in New York. The young man asked for counsel on a wide range of problems: programming, personnel, relations with government, listeners, advertisers, and other publics. We wrote policy statements for radio's and television's future. We helped bring leading figures to the air waves. We aided in publicizing an historic event: the broadcasting for the first time of the New York Philharmonic Orchestra, marking the attempt to build middle-class and upper-stratum audiences for radio. Radio then gave promise of becoming a great, constructive social force in entertainment, music, education, and public service. But the pressures of mass advertising for low priced consumer articles such as soap and cigarettes soon traded down programming to appeal to mass audiences. Radio has not met its social potential.

Dodge Motors Company of Detroit engaged us to launch a new automobile model, then considered an "epoch-making event." We arranged the first nationwide broadcast for the new Victory Six. Al Jolson, Will Rogers, and Fred and Dorothy Stone appeared on the program, and the president of Dodge spoke. Next morning Dodge showrooms all over America bulged with thousands of potential buyers who had heard the broadcast.

Another businessman for whom we acted as counsel was William B. Ward of the Ward Baking Company. He introduced the mass production of bread by mechanical means. Ingredients were fed into hoppers on the top floor and emerged on the ground floor as wrapped bread on conveyor belts leading directly to delivery trucks. Mr. Ward wanted to establish an efficient, huge bread trust. But his ambition was shattered when the Justice Department threatened an anti-trust suit and scotched the venture. During our incumbency we were his policy advisers on employment matters, on public interest ventures, and on general public policy of the company.

Vacuum Oil Company, separated from the Standard Oil Company by the historic Landis court decision, retained us as advisers. They sought to improve relations with firms in the motor industry, in shipping, in the new aviation industry, and in other oil-using industries. We aided them in encouraging the aviation industry's growth. We were associated with the first transatlantic flights from England to the United States by Kingsford Smith, as well as with ill-fated attempts such as that of René Fonck to reach Europe from the United States by air. This was a classic example of the coincidence of the private and the public interest.

We advised the famous Seligman galleries on how to gain public acceptance for Gothic art and modem art, for painters such as Modigliani, Seurat, and others. Years later we carried on comparable activities for the house of Wildenstein, art dealers. We helped fight hatlessness for the millinery industry.

Working with the unhappy Boston retailing millionaire E. A. Filene, who combined idealism with egotism, we helped promote his ideas for the extension of mass credit to workers, mass travel for the middle class, and better mass distribution for the American consumer. Many of these ideas became integral parts of the American system of labor-management relations, a tribute to Filene's pioneer thinking.

A hairnet manufacturer, Venida, asked us to increase the wearing of hairnets, then hampered by the short hair fashion introduced by dancer Irene Castle. We explored the uses of hairnets as a safety measure for women working with machinery, and as a result of public visibility of the idea, several states passed laws making it obligatory for women to wear hairnets under certain working conditions. The segmental approach was developed by stressing the sanitary aspect of hairnets for cooks and waitresses.

The diversity of organizations which engaged us appeared

limitless in the booming 1929 stock market. Public relations was thriving too. During that year, General Electric and Westinghouse decided to celebrate the fiftieth anniversary of the invention of the electric light by Thomas Alva Edison. They came to us to explore ways of demonstrating the contribution electric light made to society and to guide them in commemorating Light's Golden Jubilee on October 21, 1929. Many Americans revered the memory of Edison. Henry Ford had built at Dearborn, Michigan the Edison Institute of Technology (a replica of Independence Hall) in honor of his great inspiration, Edison. For months the anniversary was celebrated throughout the world. President Herbert Hoover, as well as dignitaries from business, finance, industry, and science (including Madame Curie) attended the culminating banquet at the Edison Institute. Walter Winchell started a rumor that I had induced the Post Office to issue a two-cent postage stamp with a picture of an electric light bulb on it. Actually the Post Office acted on its own initiative as a result of the high public visibility the Jubilee had achieved.

Leonard W. Doob described Light's Golden Jubilee as "one of the most lavish pieces of propaganda ever engineered in this country during peace time."[1] John T. Flynn wrote:

> On October 21, 1929, there occurred the climax of a celebration ostensibly designed to commemorate Edison's invention of the incandescent lamp. Edison re-enacted this procedure before a distinguished audience in Detroit which included Henry Ford and the President of the United States. Before and after this event, the praises of Edison were sung

---

1. Leonard W. Doob, *Propaganda* (New York, 1935), 195.

all over the world; the United States Government even issued a special postage stamp with the picture of an electric light upon it. Henry Ford reconstructed the village in which Edison was born, and the original laboratory where the convention had been conceived was reproduced as faithfully as possible. On the surface a truly great man was being honored by a famous industrialist. As a matter of fact, Mr. Bernays was the man who managed and directed the series of dramatic episodes. He was working "not for Edison or for Henry Ford, but for very important interests which saw in this historic anniversary an opportunity to exploit and publicize the uses of the electric light."[2]

There never had been any question as to who had sponsored the Jubilee.

In its otherwise favorable coverage of Light's Golden Jubilee, *The New Yorker* on November 9, 1929, was unwilling to accept the term "counsel on public relations." It coined a new term, "specialist in making news events."

Despite some non-acceptance of our terminology of public relations, concern with public opinion had proliferated greatly in business and other circles. Two well informed observers in 1929 estimated the number of publicity agents in New York, unattached or associated with advertising corporations. Marlen Pew of *Editor & Publisher* put the figure at 5,000. Stanley Walker, city editor of the *New York Tribune*, estimated that 5,000 covered New York and Washington.[3]

---

2. John T. Flynn, "Edward L. Bernays," *Atlantic Monthly*, Vol. 149 (1932), 564
3. Stanley Walker, "Playing the Deep Bassoons," *Harper's*, Vol. 164, 370

Obviously, the importance of attempts to influence public opinion was very considerable at end of our first decade in business.

ACTIVITIES IS THE 1930s

The next period, 1930–1941, saw depression and recovery. With the stock market crash in the fall of 1929, business dropped from the apex of the pyramid of power to the bottom. It lost much of its authority and charisma in American society. A bloodless revolution was effected by the New Deal. To meet the new conditions, business retained counsel on public relations more extensively than ever before.

As the depression continued, clients came to us in increasing numbers. President Herbert Hoover appointed me a member of his Emergency Committee for Employment, headed by my old friend Colonel Arthur Woods. Hoover, not temperamentally fitted to deal with the contemporary social disaster, tried to exorcise the depression. President Franklin Delano Roosevelt and the New Deal then swept in with new concepts and programs geared to the crisis.

Public relations firms and public relations departments in corporations proliferated in the early 1930's. For example, Carl Byoir opened his public relations office in 1930, Hill and Knowlton in 1933, and Earl Newsom in 1935. More and more large corporations set up their own public relations departments, reflecting the awareness by business of the growing importance of public relations to success in the modem economy. Sears Roebuck in 1927, Bethlehem Steel in 1930, General Motors in 1931, the Baltimore and Ohio Railroad in 1934, the Atchison, Topeka and Santa Fe Railroad in 1936, International Harvester in 1937, and the New York Central Railroad in 1939 were examples of the trend.

Other institutions also needed professional counsel on public relations. The Committee on the Cost of Medical Care, sponsored by leading foundations and headed by Ray Lyman Wilbur, retained us to help achieve its goal. On a voluntary basis we cooperated with leading economists, including Carl Snyder of the Federal Reserve System, Lionel D. Edie, Warren M. Persons, and others, to win public support for credit expansion. They believed it would return prosperity to the country. Finally, Eugene Meyer, head of the Federal Reserve Bank, helped expand the nation's credit by the purchase of United States bonds by the United States government. Snyder had made studies of America's economic history which showed that when credit expanded 4 per cent annually, prosperity was maintained.

After Prohibition's repeal in the early part of the decade, the United Brewers Industrial Foundation asked us to assist them in their reintegration into American society. We worked out a public policy platform for them. The Foundation, in enlightened self-interest, accepted our recommendation that they support the authorities in their effort to ensure that the pre-Prohibition saloon era did not return. The lasting effect of this action is still evident.

Another way in which we tried to influence public tastes was to help the book publishers to encourage the reading of books. We urged contractors and architects to build bookshelves in houses and apartments. Empty bookshelves induced book purchases.

We participated in proxy battles for control of large corporations, notably the American Aviation Company. Companies such as the Great Northern Railroad (on the initiative of the First National Bank of New York) and the City Stores Company came to us for help on their financial public relations problems brought on by the depression. Then a new field, financial public relations is now a highly specialized branch of public relations practice.

We helped other businessmen, including importers of oriental pearls. Beset by the new competition of the cultured Japanese pearl, these merchants called on us for an effort to try to reinstate the oriental pearl in public favor. A Sheik from the Isle of Pearls, Bahrein, in the Persian Gulf, came to the United States to dramatize and validate our cause.

We also continued to aid worthy social causes. The Woods School of Langhorne, Pennsylvania, at our recommendation, organized a Child Research Clinic, which pioneered in exploring facts about retarded children and bringing them to the attention of relevant publics, with far-reaching effects in this area of childcare. The Clinic gave impetus to better care of mentally deficient children in our country.

We launched for the Fred French Co. the first slum clearance development of the New Deal, financed in part by the United States— Knickerbocker Village on New York's Lower East Side. Al Smith, a former resident of the neighborhood, keynoted the occasion. With the help of economists, we launched for the *Ladies' Home Journal* during the depression a nationwide It's Up to the Women movement to stimulate consumer purchasing and help the recovery effort. The movement dramatized the part women played in our economy, a hitherto neglected fact. The *Country Gentleman*, a sister publication of the *Journal*, then retained us to build public recognition for them.

At a newsworthy cornerstone-laying we dedicated the luxurious apartment hotel, Hampshire House in New York, which we had also named. The cornerstone's engraving stressed yesterday's charm and tomorrow's convenience, pointing to new modes of urban living. Due to financial stringency, however, the structure stood unfinished for seven years. After its completion Hampshire House accelerated the trend toward apartment hotel living.

Fortune, setting precedents in business journalism, retained us to establish closer relations with its readers, its potential readers, and the general public. We sent proofs of "Arms and the Man" by Eric Hodgins, a *Fortune* article that discussed the arms traffic and the promoters of war, to Senator William Borah of Idaho who initiated an arms investigation on the basis of it. It almost stopped the private arms industry. It demonstrated the power of the printed word.

Often, we were able to pursue socially laudable goals and aid our business clients simultaneously. We helped to kill the communal drinking cup when we were retained by the Dixie Cup makers. This ushered in the era of paper cups and improved health conditions. This was a constructive example of the coincidence of public and private interest at work.

We counselled other business clients, including Allied Chemical and Dye and the Nash-Kelvinator Co. This decade saw the beginning of our long relationship with the largest chemical company in the world, Allied Chemical and Dye Corporation. We advised them on as varied problems as stock exchange relationships and sales problems. We developed programs for the greater use of American manufactured nitrates by the American farmer and fought a reigning superstition among southern farmers that only bird-made nitrates from Chile were effective. Nash-Kelvinator, a new company, asked us to help adjust their various corporate actions to their many publics. The icebox on wheels was the subject of weary jokes; at the time it was considered strange for a refrigerator manufacturer and an automobile manufacturer to merge. Few if any saw in this incongruous merger the progenitor of the later business form, the conglomerate.

Another businessman who appointed us counsel on public relations during the depression was Alfred P. Sloan, president of General Motors Corporation. Even such huge consumers' goods companies had little awareness of their dependence on public de- sires. Engineers, not consumers dominated automobile design. A brilliant innovator in the firm, Henry Weaver, asked us to intercede with Mr. Sloan to convince him to pay more attention to studies of consumer preferences made by Weaver. This initiated GM's consumer research, which served as a pattern in American industry.

I sat in on executive committee meetings which determined basic company policies and programs. In the General Motors 1932 annual report, Mr. Sloan used a paragraph I wrote stressing the importance of good relations with the public, an innovation in the industry.

Other companies followed the lead of General Motors. During these years, we were concerned with a wide variety of policies and programs ranging from employee and dealer relations to new model launchings, the Chicago Fair of 1933, government relations, and annual reports. The adoption by General Motors of public relations as a major activity influenced the growing acceptance of its broad principles and practices throughout American industry.

Expansion of radio's use in this decade presented another opportunity to attempt to make it an important cultural force. For Philco Radio and Television Corporation we attempted to raise the status of radio instruments by developing radios specially designed by Norman Bel Geddes. We organized the Radio Institute of the

Audible Arts, whose director was the distinguished music critic Pitts Sanborn. Its objectives were to develop significant programs in music, entertainment, and education. Broadcasting's commercialism finally overwhelmed the effort.

Social scientists helped us define the function of greeting cards in American society. Such cards gratified our need for gregariousness and served as morale boosters for men and women who needed psychological support. They became socially more acceptable when the manufacturers accepted our recommendations to use more sophisticated art and sentiment. Similarly, we tried to improve the public relations of producers of sporting goods. To A. G. Spalding and Company we gave the advice that in their approach to the public they should stress the fact that sport strengthens character and physical fitness.

Two important clients of the thirties were the largest bank in America, the Bank of America, and the nationally known manufacturers and servicers of pullman cars, the Pullman Company. We worked closely with the banking giant, A. P. Giannini, the Italian immigrant boy who started with a peddler's wagon and became a dominant figure in American banking. We laid out plans for acceptance by the American public of branch banking, then unpopular. We worked on programs to improve relations between the bank personnel and the people of California. After some four decades we found our program still being used. It also served other banks as a model. For the Pullman Co. we made a huge study of its public relations problems, in connection with an anti-trust suit brought by the government.

Another important client was David Sarnoff, president of

RCA. He asked us to advise his new president of NBC, Lenox Lohr. My most unforgettable experience of that relationship, which covered advice on the whole range of network broadcasting, was Mr. Sarnoff's response to my request for a chart of his organization. He responded, "We have no organization chart. This is a company of men, not of charts." My experience with the company convinced me of the necessity of defining responsibilities of individuals in a large organization.

In addition to my work for businesses, I was concerned with broader social problems. Nazism and Fascism were accelerating their nefarious propaganda in the United States in the latter part of the decade. Survival of the democratic way of life became a matter of grave concern. Viking Press published my *Speak Up for Democracy* in 1939 in a large paperback edition, a manual of public relations strategy and techniques for all Americans to oppose the then prevalent Communist and Fascist propaganda before Pearl Harbor.

Harvey Gibson, chairman of the World's Fair in New York in 1939, asked us to head its public relations. This task I did on a volunteer basis. We developed the theme that it was a living symbol of democracy. My wife coined the word "Democracity" for the central attractions, the Trylon and Perisphere.

As the decade passed, it was clear that public relations work was becoming an ever more highly visible part of American life. Authors, journalists, social critics, psychologists, sociologists, and other commentators evidenced a new interest in public relations in the 1930–1941 period. All those dependent on public understanding and support became similarly concerned. As a result of the depression and the New Deal, the public now assumed greater importance in the minds of leaders. The media gave publicity to public relations, as they had not done before.

Reference to our work appeared in the daily press, general magazines, professional and trade journals, books of fiction and non-fiction, encyclopedias, bibliographies, and on the radio. Influential periodicals such as the *Atlantic Monthly* and the *American Mercury* carried full-length profiles of me. More and more businessmen also wanted to learn how to adjust to the world on which they were dependent for their continued existence.[4] I gave many talks on public relations before business groups. A typical one occurred at the International Association of Milk Dealers. I analyzed the industry's problems and recommended a course of action. I formulated objectives, a scientific analysis of the public, suggested changes in policies, products, or services based on research. I also outlined how projection and interpretation of the industry were to be made through the channels of communication.

Financial associations asked me to explain public relations to them. For instance, at the twentieth annual convention of the Financial Advertisers Association in September 1935, I explained the need for molding public opinion. I recommended a three-point public relations program for financial institutions: (1) public education on the need for banks, (2) public education on the function of banks in words the public understands, and (3) community leadership undertaken by banks and bankers to re-establish them in the public mind through their deeds.[5] The following year the Massachusetts

---

4. Boston College Conference on Retail Distribution Proceedings, 1936, "Business Turns to Counsel on Public Relations," 39–41.
5. Financial Advertisers Association "Proceedings . . . Twentieth Annual Convention," Atlantic City, New Jersey, September 9–11, 1935, 56–65.

Bankers Association asked for a comparable program to restore favorable public opinion for banks, a program which they distributed widely.

Government also used public relations increasingly. The Bureau of the Budget, the Navy, and the Departments of State, Defense, Justice, Agriculture, and the Interior all had offices of public affairs, public relations or public information. At highest policy levels, research on public attitudes as a basis for public policy and planned approaches was general. By World War II public relations was firmly established. The war emphasized the importance of public relations and furthered its acceptance by society generally and by business.

PUBLIC RELATIONS SINCE WORLD WAR II

After war's end, many additional corporations established public relations departments. Among them were Ford Motor Company in 1946, Allis-Chalmers in 1946, the Pennsylvania Railroad in 1948, Socony-Vacuum in 1949, Gulf Oil in 1949, Chrysler Corporation in 1950, Northwestern Mutual Life Insurance Company in 1951, American Oil Company in 1952, and the Southern Pacific Railroad in 1953.[6]

Nugent Wedding of the University of Illinois showed in his timely 1950 study, *Public Relations in Business: The Study of Activities in Large Corporations*, that public relations had penetrated much of American business. Of the firms considered, 35.3 per cent accepted public relations as a two-way activity including proper policy formulation and interpretation to the public; 29.4 per cent accepted the concept of good will; 10.6 per cent agreed that public

---

6. Scott M. Cutlip and Allen H. Center, *Effective Public Relations* (New York, 1952)

relations was one aspect of the selling job, the same percentage believed it was solely a publicity activity, and 8.2 per cent held it interpreted business to the public and public to business.[7]

Business had come a long way in three decades since 1923. But there was still room for improvement. In the last twenty years, public relations has become an integral part of our system. The number of practitioners has increased. The *New York Classified Directory* listed ten public relations counselors in 1935 and 394 in 1950, a fortyfold increase in fifteen years. They occupied one column in the 1940 Directory and nine columns in 1971.

In 1960 *Business Week*[8] reported that the number of public relations practitioners increased from 1,000 in 1950 to 100,000 in 1960. In 1970 the *Public Relations Reporter* claimed that a more realistic figure would be 60,000, including everybody from practitioner to mail clerk.[9] Most of them are engaged in advising business. Some 1,350 counseling organizations function, with fifty new ones added each year. Expenditures for public relations are estimated at $2,000,000,000 a year.[10]

Public relations has improved its professional education. In 1923 I gave the first course in public relations at an institution of higher learning, New York University. Today at least eighty-nine colleges give concentrated work in public relations, and more than 300 colleges have at least one course dealing with the profession. Seven colleges offer a bachelor's degree in the field, and a like number

---

7. Nugent Wedding, *Public Relations in Business: The Study of Activities in Large Corporations* (Urbana, Ill., 1950).
8. "Public Relations Today," *Business Week* (July 2, 1950), 40–62.
9. *PR Reporter*, XII, No. 27 (July 6, 1970).
10. "Public Relations Today," 40.

offer a master's degree."[11]

The first book on public relations, my *Crystallizing Public Opinion*, was published in 1923. Today there is an extensive literature. Specialized treatment has kept pace with specialization in the practice of public relations. The field has its own weekly newsletters, among them the *Public Relations Reporter* published and edited by Robert Barbour, and the *Public Relations News* founded in 1944 by Denny and Glenn Griswold. There is a monthly, the *Public Relations Journal*, published by the Public Relations Society of America, and the *Public Relations Quarterly*.

The Public Relations Society of America with 7,000 members has tried to set standards for performance and ethics. Internationally, public relations has an International Public Relations Association with public relations associations in many countries.

In business today, public relations is a top corporate function. Social action by business is no longer a luxury. Business will change or change will be forced on it. Robert Barbour of the *Public Relations Reporter* put it succinctly. He said corporate public relations men must help management to determine priorities, plan action programs and devise and execute internal and external communications systems. They will have added responsibility, greater and more critical than previously.

Public relations should continue to grow as long as the democratic society flourishes. In a mobile, fluid society competition of ideas and things in the marketplace will continue. Validation and

---

11. See Ray E. Hiebert's monograph, *Trends in Public Relations Education, 1964–1970*, published in 1971 by the Foundation for Public Relations Research and Education in New York.

licensing of public relations practitioners by the state would ensure that the counsel's capability and character serve the public interest and profession alike. The public relations counsel of the future will be both a generalist and a specialist, oriented to an understanding of the society as a whole, rather than to only one segment of it. Educational training will emphasize the policy-making and informational functions of the profession.[12]

The ethical obligations of the practitioner are founded on the public interest. The public relations counsel should evaluate the past and present and, with the aid of social science research, project possible future trends. The public relations counsel interprets the public to his client to enable him to anticipate the future in his attitudes and actions. If he does his job properly, he serves both the private and the public interest.

---

12. Edward L. Bernays, "The Outlook for Public Relations," *Public Relations Quarterly*, X, Nos. 8 and 4 (Winter 1966), 84–88.

THE MARKETING OF
NATIONAL POLICIES

A STUDY OF WAR PROPAGANDA
(1942)

DURING THE GREAT WAR, THE NATIONS realized the necessity of selling their national aims and policies. They had special marketing problems. The attitudes and actions of their own people, of neutrals and of enemies towards them, depended to a great extent on how effectively they "sold" themselves.

They discovered that arms and armaments are not the only weapons, that ideas are weapons too. They recognized in varying degree the importance of a scientific approach to the marketing of national aims and of national policies.

From an examination of the past we can learn what the marketing policies of our own nation should be today, what we should do and what we should not do to gain acceptance for our country's aims and ideals. I shall review briefly the story of how Germany, England and the United States marketed their national aims and policies during the Great War to the people of their own countries, to the neutrals and to the enemies. I shall indicate that new developments in psychological approaches and technical media have changed national marketing policies since 1917, and I shall discuss activities being carried on in this field today in Germany, England, and the United States.

I hope to prove that a scientific approach to the problem of marketing 236 national aims and policies should be adopted in the United States. I shall make recommendations on how to meet this problem of selling our democratic ideals, ideals of freedom, equality and orderly justice.

PROPAGANDA AND THE GREAT WAR

A book published in the late twenties, *Propaganda Technique in the World War*, by Harold Lasswell, attempted to isolate the factors of marketing. This analysis was made by a social psychologist looking back over past events. Obviously, things had not been planned this way in advance. He isolated six factors:

1. Fasten the war guilt on the enemy.
2. Claim unity and victory, in the names of history and deity.
3. State war aims. In the last war, the Germans failed to do this successfully. The Allies made successful counter-propaganda out of it. Security, peace, a better social order, international laws, are given as war aims.
4. Strengthen the belief of the people that the enemy is responsible for the war, with examples of the enemy's depravity.
5. Make the public believe that unfavorable news is really enemy lies. This will prevent disunity and defeatism.
6. Follow this with horror stories. The story of the Turk who sits before a tubful of his captives' eyes was first told during the Crusades. Horror stories, says the author, should be made to sound authoritative.

George C. Bruntz's book, *Allied Propaganda and the Collapse of the German Empire in 1918*, may help us in dealing with the question. He deals with the foreign angle, but his classification of psychological techniques is applicable to the domestic situation:

1. Propaganda of enlightenment: Get true facts to the people and army of the enemy country, negating the false information they are fed by their own country.

2. Propaganda of despair: Attempt to break down the morale of the enemy by showing that death, disaster and defeat face him.

3. Propaganda of hope: Present to the enemy civilians and army a picture of a promised land, if they will only lay down their arms. President Wilson gave the Fourteen Points as America's war aims.

4. Particularist propaganda: This is aimed at factions in the opposing country and army, seeks to divide them into antagonistic groups—Catholic against Protestant, the people of Alsace-Lorraine against the Prussians in the last war.

5. Revolutionary propaganda: This is aimed at breaking down the government of the enemy from within. The propaganda by the Allies in the last war aimed at stirring up the German people against the Hohenzollerns.

All psychological warfare in the Great War, domestic and foreign, recognized the following three main elements, but there was no integrated scientific plan, as there should be today:

1. Heighten the morale—unity of your own country.
2. Weaken the morale of your enemy.
3. Win over the morale of the neutrals.

LESSONS FROM THE GREAT WAR

Even though great progress in psychological research and in technology has been made in the spreading of ideas since the Great War, there are lessons to be learned from the psychological warfare of Germany, England and our own country of that period.

German psychological warfare during the Great War demonstrated what a desultory, segmented handling of the marketing problem results in. The Germans had no total psychological approach. For instance, they paid little attention to morale on the home front. They recognized the importance of external psychological warfare. They manipulated symbols, used political Machiavellianism, sabotage, terrorism, and censorship. They tried to split off Negroes, German-Americans and other groups from the main body of Americans, blew up our factories and tried to arouse Mexico against us.

The Germans used both propaganda and censorship in foreign news control. Efforts to control foreign newspapers through false fronts were a device they used then, as today; they tried to buy the *Evening Mail* in New York, for example. Control of advertising monopolies was tried in some countries. Newspaper policy and public opinion were to be influenced through advertising control. The Germans also distributed deadly dull leaflets or pamphlets and heavy academic books in foreign countries by mail. Distribution of material over enemy lines by airplane was an effective method in Italy and Russia.

After the Great War, the Germans recognized that, from a technical stand-point, their foreign propaganda was poor—too tactless, too open, too obvious, lacking in enthusiasm and "inflammatory catchwords." It antagonized more than it persuaded, and proved to be a boomerang.

In 1933, one year after Hitler's rise in power, Ewald Banse, Professor of Military Science at Brunswick Technical College, in *Germany Prepares for War*, pointed to these failures. He complained of glaring mistakes, "a lack of comprehensive thinking; thinking in terms of continents and oceans," "an ignorance of economics and of national psychology plus inadequate preparations for war, both as regards food supply, raw materials, and psychological equipment," "inadequate psychological preparation of the German government." "The stab in the army's back by which our fate was sealed," was due to these, he wrote.

The conflict between military and civilian authority on the home front added to the German difficulty until, finally, their lack of morale brought despair and collapse. The Germans studied their failures in psychological warfare after the Great War and came to recognize the importance of ideas as weapons.

The British experience in building and breaking down morale also points the way for us. The English at no time harnessed the intellectual civilian resources of the country and their knowledge of human relations to master the problem of psychological warfare on a broad integrated basis of marketing their aims and ideals.

British propaganda at home started with unofficial independent committees and groups, with no regard to the basic principles of mass psychology, and also with no integrated approach.

Wellington House, a propaganda bureau for the British Government, was principally concerned with news purveying and publications. In its work out of England, it did make a contribution. It emphasized the group leader approach, personal correspondence with influential people, it arranged for the interchange of visitors, personal tours of leaders to neutral and allied countries, visits of distinguished neutrals and representatives of the Allies to England. It won leaders who influenced large groups.

Even Lord Beaverbrook, who was put in charge of the Ministry of Information in 1918, working with Lord Northcliffe at Crewe House and with the National War Aims Committee, never got started on the total psychological warfare approach we know today. The British did have an advantage in radio and control of trans-Atlantic cables which enabled them to catch up with the better organized German propaganda in this country. Also, British propaganda dropped from airplanes in enemy countries was a potent weapon, providing a deluge of "English poison raining down from God's clear sky," to quote a German opinion—a means of reaching the public of enemy countries.

After the last war, the Germans credited the British with effective foreign propaganda. "We are bound to admit," said Banse, the German, in 1933, "that the English campaign of lies was one of the most effectual weapons used against us, conducted on thoroughly sound psychological lines. The English propaganda was run entirely by civilians, the German by soldiers." "The latter," adds Mr. Banse, "is the wrong way, because it is not the soldier's but the psychologist's opinion that counts here." We can safely say of the British as of the Germans that they recognized that they had weapons in the use of ideas, but that they never really learned how to use them effectively as an organized instrument of the national interest.

Both the Germans and English failed to use public relations activities broadly. They used censorship and propaganda as separate weapons to accomplish specific purposes. At no time, as far as I know, did they apply to psychological warfare the strategy they applied to physical warfare. They achieved unified fronts in military strategy not in psychological strategy.

The British did recognize the potency of group leaders, and of enlisting the aid of civilians such as the publishers, Northcliffe and Beaverbrook. But like the Germans they missed the importance of welding the new weapons together and, in working out a program, neglected to utilize existing knowledge of persuasion and suggestion, from among the civilian population.

THE AMERICAN FRONT

In the United States, psychological activity evolved slowly from the need for it, rather than from advance planned activity undertaken as part of a program of national defense. It did not represent a plan with definite goals, with effective strategy, and timing worked out in advance.

The Committee on Public Information, founded on April 13, 1917, did a splendid job within these limitations. I became associated with it soon after it was established and served with it here and at the Peace Conference. It did not proceed on a definitely formulated plan in its work of "holding fast the inner lines," although it did utilize some of the available knowledge of psychology and sociology. The men in it went ahead with enthusiasm on a widespread front. When anyone of us got a bright idea, it was very likely to be accepted. I remember one day suggesting that all exporters should be asked to put inserts in their letters about America's. war aims and ideals, and henceforth they did as a matter of voluntary cooperation.

The Committee distributed millions of pamphlets, spoke through advertising to the entire country, used every available means of communication, and won public opinion to war aims and ideals, in other countries as well as in our own. The organization grew and spread to all parts of the world.

The C.P.I. had 14 divisions, working together in more or less coordinated fashion. Of course there were divisions of Pictorial Publicity, Cartoons, Syndicate Features, and Foreign Press. Tremendous amounts of material were produced and widely distributed in which a definite attempt was made at adaptation to various publics. Four Minute Men spoke in movie houses and wherever audiences of any kind were assembled. Women's and Junior divisions were developed, and the activity expanded until 75,000 speakers were participating. Four Minute Men, with the Speaking Division, which handled longer talks, were the "spearhead of the assault on indifference and apathy." They reached an estimated total audience of 400,000,000, and did the job radio does today.

The Division of Films and Pictures did effective pioneer work.

The Division of Civic and Educational Cooperation produced and distributed 75,000,000 pieces of literature, bringing about, someone said, a "veritable mobilization of the country's scholarly resources, and making schools, colleges, and various non-educational groups among the strongest of strong points in the inner lines."

The work of the Divisions of Industrial Relations, Labor

Publications, and Work with the Foreign Born indicates considerable understanding of approaches, which we can handle in a much more scientific way today. It did the most effective job of all the war agencies with comparable interests, and did it democratically, without threat, intimidation, and with only voluntary censorship.

The United States shot paper bullets over the enemy lines in the World War Confidential Army reports of the period state: "The Germans have issued an order punishing with death the retention by their soldiers of any examples of American or Allied propaganda."

But even though I regard the U. S. effort as effective in marketing our war aims and ideals to America and the world on a democratic basis of suggestion and persuasion, in perspective I see it as a pioneer effort with trial and error, with much fumbling, and not as a well planned activity. Candidates for jobs were chosen on the basis of their enthusiasm for the cause, not their training and experience. There never was a chart drawn in advance for the Committee on Public Information that I know of.

CHANGES SINCE 1917

How has the situation changed since 1917? Technical means for spreading ideas have been improved, the number of channels for their distribution increased, speed of transmission tremendously accelerated, the costs of disseminating greatly lessened. In 1917, the talking movie, the radio, and the airplane, as we know them today, did not exist.

As a result of these things, leaders recognized the greater potency of the common man in the shaping of political destinies. From the French Revolution in the late 18th century through the 19th century, the power of the common man was growing. At the beginning of the 20th century, belief in his strength grew. After the Great War, self-seeking men capitalized on the fact that the common man had been swayed in the war by propaganda. This powerful common man could be influenced by symbols, by words, pictures and actions. Appeals could be made to his prejudices, his loves and his hates, to his unfulfilled desires. Manipulation of symbols by unscrupulous leaders against a background of post-war psychological and economic uncertainty led millions to follow new leaders and ideologies in the 'twenties and 'thirties. The historical truth of the development of the power of the common man, coincidental with the development of the technological methods of spreading ideas, must not be lost sight of in the treatment of these marketing problems.

The rise of Communists, Nazis, and Fascists obviously was accelerated by this manipulation of symbols through the speeded-up technical methods of spreading ideas. A symbol is a short cut to our understanding of goals. Hitler used symbolism. The Hitler salute is political symbolism. Civil servants, national, state, and local, were ordered to raise their arm in the Heil salute, immediately after Hitler gained power; then Dr. Frick, Minister of the Interior, got trade and industry to follow suit. In 1934 an official communique closed with the following sentences: "The spirit of true national community in the national socialist state and the willing identification with it implies that the whole population complies with this regulation."

The symbol of the new Germany, the swastika flag, was stressed. "There must be no house which does not display the sign of Nationalist Socialist Germany," was printed on a handbill signed by the local group of the national socialist party and placed in every mailbox the day of the plebescite on Germany's withdrawal from the League of Nations. The Fuehrer himself is the most powerful symbol. A book published in 1933 in Germany on Propaganda and National Might says: "No passion, no idea can find its final and strongest expression without this great symbol." The National Ministry of Public Enlightenment and Propaganda with Dr. Goebbels as its director and with 31 regional agencies made full use of these symbols, and ground them continually into the consciousness of the common man to lure him closer to Nazism. Russia and Italy used somewhat similar approaches.

Knowledge of the human mind, and of human relations has greatly increased since 1917. Sociologists, psychologists, social psychologists, theoretical and practical experts in public opinion have studied principles and techniques since the War. Public Relations has emerged as a new field. In 1922 there was no course in public relations that I know of in any American university. I gave the first one in 1923 at New York University. A recent study we made shows that 31 universities were offering 68 courses in Public Relations, Public Opinion, and related subjects, and these figures have probably increased since our survey. In fact, Doris E. Fleischman and I coined the expression "counsel on public relations" to define this new field of activity.

Since 1917, we know much more about the working of the human mind. We know that acceptance of ideas comes through feeling, reason, custom, authority, persuasion and factual evidence. Industries and governments call upon advisers on public opinion. We use measurement techniques to determine how far private interest conforms to public desires. A baker now only bakes the bread he knows his public will buy. On the other hand, organized persuasion often changes attitudes of the public and leads it to new actions.

THE ENGINEERING APPROACH

All these factors—and the experience of the Great War—led to the engineering approach to the problem—the engineering of consent in a democracy. What do I mean by this? I mean that problems of public relations are handled as an engineer plans the building of a bridge, or as a tactician works out a military campaign. What are our goals? What are we selling? What are our aims? What is the time factor? Have we the men and materials we need?

When we know what our goal is, we make a study of public opinion to appraise our problem. What are the limits of tolerance of the public? What symbols—words, pictures and actions—are effective in changing public attitudes and actions? What are the channels of communication through which to reach the public with these symbols? What is the group formation of the public we are reaching? How much in men, money and materials is required?

After we have learned all these things, we can work out strategy, planning, and timing, in an engineering approach to our objectives. Segmented attack may be of some little value, but integration and unified attack are fundamental.

Every approach must be used to affect every kind of attitude as part of a broad integrated program, giving the proper relationship to each element, just as in military affairs the able army is the one that balances its weapons effectively to meet its goals.

This approach to public relations can be used for social ends, or can be abused for unsocial ones. It can be carried out on a democratic basis of suggestion and persuasion or on an undemocratic basis of suppression, threat, intimidation, and brutality. This engineering approach to public opinion should be applied in a democratic way to U. S. wartime pursuits as it is to peacetime pursuits.

As early as 1927, after he had made his authoritative study, *Propaganda Technique in the World War,* Lasswell wrote that propaganda had become a profession. "The modern world," he wrote, "is busy developing a corps of men who do nothing but study the ways and means of changing minds or binding minds to their convictions. Propaganda is developing its practitioners, its professors, its teachers and its theories. It is to be expected that governments will rely increasingly upon the professional propagandists for advice and aid."

How are England, Germany, and our own country using the instruments and knowledge available for total psychological warfare?

England certainly has not learned much from the experience of the last war or taken account of the changes and developments of the intervening years. The handling of public relations in England during the first part of the war was astonishingly inept. Criticism of censorship and other activities brought about changes in management. Even today there is much left undone both in domestic and foreign activity.

Britain's morale is maintained despite her public relations techniques. As an example, here is a recent United Press report: "*The Daily Mirror* today attacked Colonel Walter Elliott, Director of Public Relations at the War Office, as a 'fool who should keep his folly to himself. Speaking at Manchester yesterday he had the impertinence to accuse the British people of lacking guts,' the *Mirror* said. 'Elliott obviously knows nothing about the average man or woman. He should go around to some of the blitzed towns immediately after a raid. He must not go about the country insulting them and he should not be allowed to direct anything, least of all public relations.'" Bad British public relations have adversely affected the domestic and foreign situation despite Churchill's and Bevin's changes for the better.

While Britain has not profited from her experiences in the last war, Germany has. Since then, Germany has been working on psychological rearmament—adding Nazi schrecklichkeit, of course. Her scientists have studied and written about national psychology, psychological warfare, psychological espionage, the psychology of military life.

Ewald Banse's recommendations made in 1933, were translated into action by the Nazis. They even went further, not only rectifying their mistakes, but building up a monster system of forcing morale by dictatorship.

The Nazis with totalitarian brutality centralized all the machinery of idea formation into a Ministry for National Enlightenment and Propaganda. To persuasion and suggestion they added brutality, threat, intimidation and censorship. All negative viewpoints were eliminated by one or more devices to bring about an enforced "national unity."

Besides supervision of the press, broadcasting, films, music, art and the theatre, the Ministry includes general information on home policy; the organization of national holidays and festivals; tourist and economic propaganda; the organization of art exhibitions, films and sports in foreign countries. All State and Party meetings, conferences and receptions also come within its sphere. The Ministry is both the stage manager and the loudspeaker of the Nazi regime. Under it the press is subject to the most stringent regulations and close organization ever achieved in any country. Journalists must be registered, and the Press Association is a statutory body under the Minister of Propaganda. Newspaper proprietorship and shareholdings are rigorously controlled, and no joint stock company, cooperative society of public or learned body of any kind may publish a newspaper.

Here we have the totalitarian apotheosis of morale building carried on in total psychological warfare—offensive and defensive. Only the Nazis practiced this advance building of morale at home— false and demagogic though it was. And abroad they carried on similarly, applying the knowledge they had acquired in what we call the strategy of terror.

WHERE WE STAND TODAY

Where do we stand in relation to our own morale—what lessons can we learn? Certainly we must recognize the potency of ideas, ably handled, as weapons of offense and defense. We have been geared for peacetime activities; we function by adjustment arrived at through democratic processes. We accommodate conflicting viewpoints in evolutionary progress. We want no dictatorial authority to abuse power and the people. We must recognize in dealing with our own morale that we have recently passed through years of depression. This has left its mark on millions suffering from economic and psychological insecurity. We all have a great yearning for security and for realization of the ideals of democracy. Equality, freedom, orderly justice, opportunity, and security have not been completely achieved.

We have also been exposed to divisive propaganda from within and without. We have the best way of life and government yet devised. Our democracy has ideals of freedom, equality, opportunity. But they have not been effectively presented in symbols to all the people.

Our people have already provided billions of dollars for physical armies and armaments. Through their elected representatives they have voted for the first peacetime selective service army in the life of the nation. If we are to be fully prepared for whatever may come, we shall have to convince the people that psychological ramparts in this country must be as strong as our physical ramparts. Such belief must be founded on greater economic and psychological security for the individual, on a strengthening of democracy and the democratic faith. Such belief, based on an understanding of our aims, will express itself in a will to victory and to sacrifice.

To achieve it effectively is our goal. There is urgency and need— and we have the country with us. Now we can plan. All of us can help build this morale through effective marketing policies. Here are concurrent programs of action with the objective of building morale through a balanced public relations effort.

ELEMENTS OF A UNIFIED ATTACK

All of us can play a part in this program; but leadership by our government is essential for the effective carrying out of the program. Only a unified attack on the whole problem can lead to the best result. First, harness the soundest intellectual resources of the country for a psychological general staff to be called upon for advice by government; second, construct a program to strengthen faith in democracy; and third, build a program to strengthen democracy itself.

Every government and private organization, carrying on any activity that impinges on morale, can fit into such a broad program.

First, the Government needs a psychological general staff to advise on all major questions of morale—in industry, civilian life, army and navy. This staff would provide the soundest available knowledge for building morale and for psychological warfare-and by having on tap the ablest technicians, would speed up the entire morale building processes. Such a moral commission in its field of psychological defenses would take its place on a parity with the general staff in physical defenses.

Much good work is now being done in this field by public relations divisions of many government departments—Army, Navy, and the others—but as far as I have been able to find out, *there is no master plan* worked out by technicians drawn from the fields of the social sciences, sociology, psychology, ethnology, adult education, economics, the Army, Navy, public opinion, communications, public relations and market research. There are available in this country today many individuals in these fields whose experience, aptitudes, and skills fit them admirably for such advisory activity.

Technicians already advise government on many subjects. There should be a master plan of psychological approaches, just as there is a master plan for physical defense. A psychological general staff should advise on methods and procedures to meet the national goals that have been set up by government. It should not make policy but it should advise on how to put policy into practice efficiently and democratically. Many governmental and private bureaus are carrying on activities to build morale. But is it not obvious that all these morale activities might better receive a broad orientation from a group of experts working closely with those who carry out national policy? This will give the broad, important, overall psychological situation the same kind of attention the general staff gives to planning to achieve military objectives. It is important that this organization should not be a propaganda bureau, not a publicity bureau. It is to be a planning, strategy and advisory body. It should have no authority except the authority that is inherent in good advice.

Second, a program to strengthen faith in democracy. We can get people to understand democracy better by getting them to see the true alternatives between it and Nazism and Fascism. Everyone can speak up for democracy, can tell those he comes in contact with by word of mouth and in other ways what its goals and realities are. Such activity, undertaken in a broad way as a national program of public education, under the leadership of government or private individuals, must be one step in creating a dynamic will for democracy instead of a passive acceptance of it. Millions of Americans are willing to be eager proponents for democracy.

Third, a program to strengthen democracy. By strengthening democracy I mean making democracy work better, making its ideals come true—working individually or as groups to help bring about the ideals of liberty, equality and orderly justice, which (we might as well face it) do not exist for all at present. That means using our influence to increase security, opportunities, education. Our aims and ideals must be set. A happy healthy person has a strong morale. We can help to make Americans happy by strengthening democracy. Government is doing this already, but government in a democracy depends on the people. The people—and the leaders of the people— must work to strengthen democracy.

Experts, including marketing men, have laid a sound basis for a scientific approach to the problem of psychological warfare in the crisis we face today. The Nazis have translated this knowledge into action for their own evil ends. America should not, cannot wait. She must apply today what she already knows towards meeting the problems she faces.

The Press Must Act to Meet
Postwar Responsibility
(1944)

COMMUNICATIONS TODAY AND IN THE POSTWAR world constitute a problem of vital concern.

First, what are the public relations policies and practices that govern American daily newspapers today?

Second, what are the attitudes of the American people toward the daily press today?

Third, what are the issues and goals the American people are interested in now and for the postwar period?

The press, radio, motion pictures and magazines are our four greatest media of communication. They bear tremendous social responsibility in a transitional period when our democracy has basic decisions to make which will determine what the future shall be. Each of these media has the same obligation. This obligation must not only be fulfilled but must also be recognized by the public as having been fulfilled.

The daily press has made enormous strides in the last few years. The English language newspapers of the country reached an all-time high circulation of 44,392,839 copies a day during 1943, despite a decline in the number of dailies to a new low mark of 1,754. The rise in circulation over 1942 was 1,017,979 copies a day, as shown by figures compiled by *Editor & Publisher*. Foreign language papers published in the United States accounted for an additional daily circulation of approximately 1,366,000 copies.

The press has made wide gains reportorially, too. It is now covering the civilian and military activities of the nation and the rest of the world on a scope scarcely dreamed of before Pearl Harbor. It is doing this despite delivery problems and the shortage of newsprint and manpower.

But the press, as I shall show, has failed to gain the broad public acceptance it should, either as a disseminator of news or as an instrument of social leadership, the two functions of a free and independent press in a democracy. There is danger to our democratic well-being in this condition, for unless the public regards the press as a free and independent gazette and an instrument of leadership, it will find difficulty in maintaining its status and privileges in our society. It may lose its position as a public service institution, and there may be a tendency on the part of the public toward restriction, control and economic pressure, despite the First Amendment.

I have come to these conclusions from a study of authoritative surveys and from personal correspondence with publishers all over the nation. I present them because problems vitally affecting both the public and the press are involved.

Most newspapers have platforms which exist in the mind of the management, are expressed in the editorial columns or appear in printed form under the masthead of the editorial page or in some other part of the paper. Since statements of the actual platforms of papers and their policies were not available, I set out to get them. One hundred sixty-nine publishers of American daily newspapers in 161 cities, in forty-three states where 96 per cent of the dailies are located, cooperated by providing the information I needed. The newspapers I studied were approximately 9 per cent of the entire daily press of America, based on the number of daily newspapers—1,754 reported by *Editor & Publisher*—a cross-section of the entire press.

Eighteen per cent of these newspapers state their platforms in their mastheads. Seventeen per cent state them in other parts of the paper. Sixty-three per cent outlined their public relations policies or platforms to me in letters. In only four cases, less than 2 per cent, was no platform stated.

Publishers of these 169 representative newspapers, large and small, from all over the country were in correspondence with me— the *Atlanta Constitution,* the *Bloomington* (Ill.) *Pantograph,* the *Boston Globe,* the *Detroit News,* the *Lansing State Journal,* the *Louisville Times,* the *Milwaukee Journal,* the *New York Times,* the *San Francisco Chronicle,* the *Shreveport Times,* the *St. Louis Post-Dispatch,* the *Tulsa Tribune,* the *Walla Walla Union-Bulletin* and the *Wilmington Delaware Star.* Answers varied. Many of my correspondents entered into a discussion of their platforms and cited methods used to implement platforms—campaigns and crusades.

We shall appraise newspapers and their platforms from two standpoints: first, as a professional service purveying news, an informant of public opinion, independent and free; second, as a social instrument of leadership expressing itself in interest in the local community—in improvements, projects, cooperation; and in interest in the national government—in patriotism, in war and postwar interests.

Newspapers on the whole do not stress political party alignments in their platforms. Of the 169 papers covered, 68 per cent do not mention their political party at all. Eighteen per cent say that they are completely independent. Four per cent state they are Republican but independent, and 1 per cent Democratic but independent. This makes 23 per cent of the newspapers that emphasize political independence. Added to the 68 per cent that do not mention politics in their platforms, this makes a total of 91 per cent stressing either no political alignment or independence. Only 9 per cent—4 per cent Republican and 5 per cent Democrat—report definite party affiliations.

One publisher said, "Politically we are Republican, but we are not abusive of the other side." Another used almost identical wording: "We are Republican in politics, but we do not abuse or throw mud at other parties." Still another replied, "Our politics is independent Democratic but, having no opposition party newspaper here, we do not 'leg' on politics at all."

Of the 169 newspapers, 18 per cent place their chief emphasis in platforms on their services as news purveyors, 34 per cent mainly on local planks, 20 per cent on local and news purveying planks, 12 per cent on local and national planks, 5 per cent mainly on national issues, 7 per cent on national, local and news purveying planks, 4 per cent on national and news purveying planks.

Looking at the entire field, the platforms of 73 per cent reflect little if any interest in national affairs. Only 5 per cent stress national affairs as of prime importance. Seventy-four per cent mention local planks.

Listing the methods used to accomplish their particular

platforms, 48 per cent of the papers stress news policy, 41 per cent editorial policy, 13 per cent special services and 4 per cent campaigns. The platforms are broken down in my study, by geographical areas— Northeast, Southeast, South Central, North Central and Pacific sections. But space does not allow details. I shall try to hit the high spots.

Platforms cited here are described in words taken from the letters of publishers who responded in this poll on their policies and practices. As disseminator of news, planks or slogans in all areas emphasized "accuracy," "impartiality," "fairness," "thorough coverage," "dependability," "all the news," "research for facts," "non-partisan," "unbiased," "clarity," "sincerity," "honesty," "justice," "truthfulness," "reliability," "helpfulness," "courageous," "tolerance," "loyalty."

Independence and freedom were stressed throughout in many different ways. The following phrases are representative: "A policy without fear or favor," "presenting all sides," "no dictation," "against injustice," "progressive," "liberal," "independent," "impartial," "a free press." There is general agreement in the platforms on independence and freedom.

Local planks, often repetitious, run through 74 per cent of these platforms. Here are some high spots: "Improving local schools," "sewers," "streets," "roads," "city manager government," "parks," "recreation," "community welfare," "church support," "farm," "luncheon clubs," "local taxes," "recreational buildings," "full use of port facilities," "best rail and air service," "comfort stations for shoppers," "noise abatement," "flood control," "improved transit facilities," "house numbering," "advancement of prestige as art center" and hundreds of other local causes.

In the last division, national interest or patriotism, we find conformity of thinking expressed in such phrases as: "Don't lose faith in America," "interest of America above party," "to interpret and criticize salient news on government," "friend and defender of persecuted and oppressed," "inviolability of human rights," "cooperation with government," "our country right or wrong."

As to war and postwar planks, and there are only a few of these, here are representative ones: "A united local citizenry to carry out postwar prosperity planning," "to make tomorrow better than today for a new world," "interpretation—information—aggressive leadership." There was a scattering of "decentralizing the government," "states' rights," the "republic against democracy," from Southern, Middle West and Pacific points. So much for the platforms.

Now as to the second set of facts. What does the public think of newspapers? A comprehensive study of this question was made by the editors of *Fortune* in 1939. I checked with the editors of *Fortune* only a few days ago to inquire whether these figures still held. They told me their data have been continually checked since then, that the figures remain on the whole authentic and that the trend shown by them has been continuing.

This *Fortune* study sought to learn where the public got its news, whether they believed it to be accurate, free from prejudice, fair, whether they believed it is influenced by advertisers, by friends or foes of the public, and whether government should control the newspapers.

Where does the public get its news? More than 60 per cent give newspapers as the primary source. Forty per cent of the nation finds that it can get and does get its news without turning to the newspapers.

One quarter relies chiefly on the radio for news. In this one quarter are twice as many of the poor as the prosperous. Newspapers are most popular in the Northeast; radio is more popular on the Pacific coast.

Which does the better job of supplying news, the newspaper or the radio? The public was divided as to which of these mediums gave the news more accurately, 38.3 per cent voting for the newspapers and 39 per cent for the radio; 49 per cent were of the opinion the radio was free from prejudice and only 17 per cent backed the newspapers on this question. *The higher the economic bracket*, the higher the regard for the press. Seventy-nine and three one-hundreds per cent felt the newspaper gave the news to them more fully.

To the question "Which do you like best, newspaper editorials, newspaper columnists or radio commentators?" radio was the country's preferred source of news interpretation, a total of 39.3 per cent choosing radio commentators, 25.9 per cent newspaper editorials and 10.7 per cent newspaper columnists. Radio is the public's preferred source of news interpretation, it would appear from this.

"If you heard conflicting versions of the same story from these sources, which would you be most likely to believe?" Answers here show a weak hold on the public of the editorial writer and columnist: 40.3 per cent would be most likely to believe the radio press bulletin or commentator, 26.9 per cent the newspaper editorialist's news item or columnist, 11.6 per cent said it depended on the writer or speaker.

"How accurate is the press? In your experience, do newspaper headlines usually give you an accurate idea of what happened?" Fifty-nine and one-tenth per cent say "yes," 29.4 per cent "a misleading idea." Only 45.1 per cent believe the news story is usually accurate.

"Is the press fair? Do the newspapers provide fair and unprejudiced news about controversial subjects?" Those who felt the newspapers did not give fair and unprejudiced news on politics and politicians totaled 45.9 per cent, on labor 31.4 per cent, on business and businessmen 25.9 per cent, on foreign affairs 20.1 per cent, on religion and racial problems 15.5 per cent.

On the question "Do you believe that the newspapers you read soft-pedal news that is unfavorable to friendly politicians?" about 50 per cent believed "yes," about 50 per cent believed "yes" relative to friends of the publisher, about 40 per cent "yes" relative to big advertisers, about 29 per cent "yes" concerning business in general and about 22 per cent "yes" relative to labor unions.

The answers collectively, when we take those that say "in some cases" into account, show distrust on the part of the readers towards their newspapers. There is a majority in every section of the country, in every occupation and income group, that believes its publishers can be reached by politicians, friends, advertisers and business.

"Is the press freer?" The majority believes it is—63.4 per cent. The minority which does not believe the press is free says that it has been prevented from being free: 22.9 per cent by newspaper owners, 19.6 per cent by politicians, 15.7 per cent by capitalists, 12.5 per cent by government, 11.3 per cent by advertisers. To the question "Do you think that newspapers should have the right of honest criticism about a book, a movie, the quality of a brand of gasoline, the labor policy of an employer, the way a company operates its business?" a large majority believes the press has more rights than it now customarily exercises.

Certainly these findings which, the editors of *Fortune* say, have continued to reflect against the newspaper since 1939, indicate that there is a great gap between the platforms of the newspapers and public acceptance of them, particularly in the field of news dissemination, freedom and independence. If we start with the premise that the public does not accept the press now, and follow it through to its logical conclusion, what will be the condition in the postwar era? The implication for the newspapers, the public and our democracy is dark, indeed!

Every consideration of the national interest demands that this situation be altered; it cannot be permitted to remain as it is. The problem is not getting any easier to solve and, if we are to accept what the *Fortune* survey shows, it is growing more difficult.

Let us quickly run over the third set of facts.

What are the issues with which the people of America are concerned now and for the postwar period? The question must be asked and the answer given before we come to specific public relations recommendations to the newspapers. Newspaper public relations platforms must be reconciled with public attitudes and democratic goals if the newspaper is to have the place in our society it deserves.

The National Planning Association published recently the findings of polls made by the Office of Public Opinion Research, Princeton University. Briefly what America wants is this: All income groups want cooperative national planning by business, including agriculture, labor and government. America believes the government is responsible for seeing to it that everyone who wants to work has a job. It demands certain social reforms in the field of social security— old age insurance 94 per cent, job insurance 89 per cent, health insurance 85 per cent, aid for students 79 per cent. It wants a central government agency with inclusion of representatives of business, labor and agriculture with authority to guide domestic policy as to reemployment, plant conversion, demobilization. It wants educational help and job opportunities for the returning soldiers. It wants food rationing continued for a period after the war, if this is necessary to feed the peoples in devastated countries.

A survey conducted recently by Elmo Roper, and published in the *American Mercury*, shows that the American worker who makes up a great part of our country wants security, a chance to advance himself, a recognition of his status as an individual American and his personal contribution to America and the next generation.

We have examined the three sets of facts. What are our conclusions and recommendations?

If the newspaper effectively serves the public as a news disseminator and a social instrument, we do not need to be concerned about the newspaper as a successful private enterprise. Circulation and advertising follow if the newspaper is integrated with the public, and the public with the newspaper, just as today circulation and advertising often are the results of causes that have little or no relationship to the press as a social instrument or a news disseminator.

Our recommendations obviously apply to the daily newspaper field as a whole. They do not refer to any individual newspaper.

Newspapers must act on the basic consideration that a democracy needs a free and independent press which disseminates accurate, complete news and is also a social instrument of leadership for constructive improvement. Newspapers may have much advertising and circulation brought about by many different causes today, but if they do not act on this basic consideration they will not be able to maintain their position in our society.

Newspapers must make a realistic re-examination of their public relations platforms. Here are our recommendations for platforms explaining the newspapers as a vocal instrument of leadership:

Greater emphasis should be placed on national and international social goals in the platforms of American newspapers. Planks of local character, emphasizing physical improvements in a community, now so generously used, might be reconsidered and re-shaped.

Greater emphasis might be placed on promoting local social goals, consistent, of course, with national and international social goals. The American people are vitally interested in postwar jobs, social reforms, social security, educational and other aid for returning soldiers, a chance to advance themselves, a recognition of their personal contribution to America and to the next generation. Planks of this kind, it seems to me, might receive emphasis on a local as well as national basis. These suggestions are not intended to deprecate or minimize local matters in any way. Local projects are important, local issues are vital to our well-being and happiness.

As to planks of a news disseminating character, these are well stated by the newspapers of the country. But it is apparent that what they stand for is not as acceptable to the public as it ought to be. Newspapers, to maintain their status, must not only adhere to these planks, they must also make a vigorous avowal of them to the public. These planks must be continually "sold" to the public in every possible way.

In the leadership field, the press can develop vigorous campaigns for action. Newspapers in the past have demonstrated this leadership technique by sponsoring crusades for one cause or another. Colonial papers fought the Stamp Act. Noah Webster's *Minerva* in 1793 began the fight, joined by many others, against slavery. The old *New York World*'s crusade against the Ku Klux Klan is famous. The *St. Louis Post-Dispatch* uncovered the Teapot Dome scandal in the national government. The New York *Times* and the New York *Herald Tribune* sponsor annual current events forums of international importance.

In the news disseminating field, the press must not alone stand for freedom from prejudice but must "sell" this freedom from prejudice to the public. It can accomplish this in one respect by special feature articles to appeal to each racial and religious group within the paper's scope of influence. It can make rapid strides by further eliminating the racial angle from crime stories.

It must "sell" to the public constantly that it is truthful and accurate, particularly in those areas in which the public appears to doubt its fairness—its treatment of politicians and politics, labor and labor leaders, business and businessmen, and foreign affairs as well as religious and racial problems. It must stress to the public in every way its independence from domination by newspaper owners, politicians, capitalists, government or advertisers. The press must consciously go about trying to make the public recognize its values in the fields of leadership and news.

This can be done through what is known as the "engineering of consent," using public relations procedures employed today by all kinds of groups, to gain greater acceptance for the press from the public. This activity covers a knowledge of maladjustments with the public, and their elimination; of objectives, themes, strategy, timing, planning, organization and the use of tactics, through every channel of approach to win the public over.

Democracy needs a free and independent press as a news disseminating instrument and as a force for social leadership. The press, in order to maintain its status and fulfill these functions, must give serious thought to the situation it finds itself in—and act to change it, in its own and the public interest.

Public Education for Democracy
(1938)

TODAY, DEMOCRACY IS CHALLENGED ON ALL SIDES. It is the obligation of all those who are interested in democracy to do all in their power to strengthen it in order to preserve it. This demands the building up of an inner bulwark of dynamic belief and confidence in our democracy by all the people.

Freedom of self-expression is the essence of democracy. This freedom has been guaranteed by our American Constitution, in the Bill of Rights. It includes freedom of speech, of assembly, of the press, of petition, of religion. These freedoms in themselves create conflicts of opinion. Freedom of opinion is, therefore, an important element in democracy.

Those who believe in democracy have in the past been content to let the democratic processes themselves be the best protection against assault. Not until recently has our democracy been assailed from within and from without, by opinions contrary to it. It is part of our democratic American heritage to abhor censorship. We must see to it, therefore, that the wall against which the anti-democratic missiles are hurled is strong and impregnable, capable of standing firm against any onslaught. If we are to maintain the democracy upon which our system rests, we must depend upon the acceptance and defense of democracy by all the people. Democracy cannot be taken for granted. It must be cherished as a vital force. The people must be made to understand it, so that, fully aware of its real values to them in every phase of their lives, they may be ready and eager to fight for its maintenance.

Of course, the very processes of democracy work toward these ends through universal education, through our political institutions, and through the exercise of civil liberties. But the present situation which faces us requires more. To build up a powerful offensive within the body politic, ready to stand for what it believes and to combat anti-democratic viewpoints that assail it, we must go further. Naturally, we must rely on education and our other basic institutions. But in these critical times we must, in addition, make use of all the available socially sound methods to help in the upholding of our democracy. Our people must be taught its true values, its meaning to them in the continuance of what they hold dear.

To engage in this task of public education, we must understand how to reach the people with democracy's message, how to tell them what democracy means, so that they will understand it and appreciate it. Lip service to democracy is not enough. It must be implemented by the will and action of the people to preserve democracy at all costs.

MEANS OF COMMUNICATION

Science provides means of bringing men together, as well as keeping men apart. They are used on every hand to keep men apart. Modern science and inventions have spun an unbelievably close web of all kinds of communication through which ideas reach us and which can bring us all closer together for democracy. To maintain democracy, we must be aware of the facts and the implications of this network of communication to which practically every American is exposed. Only a deaf man or a blind one or a completely inaccessible one is free from the impressions and the opinions that come to him through the press, the telegraph, the cable, the radio, pamphlets, articles, letters, leaflets, sound pictures, the newsreels, the printed word, the spoken word, in all media—or through the broad forums that groups of Americans provide for the spoken and written word.

Let us look at some figures in this network in the United States: Of newspapers and periodicals we have over 25,000; the aggregate circulation of our Sunday papers is about 31,000,000, and of our daily papers, over 41,000,000; there are approximately 700 commercial radio stations; American families have some 26,000,000 radio sets; there are 16,000 moving picture theaters, with an average weekly attendance of 115,000,000; there are 260,000 billboards; 9,000 new books were published last year. One need merely indicate these figures to realize the opportunities this network offers to those who would lead men's minds towards democracy or away from it. By and large, both the friends and the enemies of democracy spread their message through the same media—through the press, through the radio, through the printed and the spoken word.

Let us consider for a moment just a few of the groups that are ready to spread democracy. There are approximately 16,000 women's clubs in the country; 2,200 chambers of commerce; of patriotic groups, the American Legion alone has 11,000 units; there are 1,500 college alumni groups; 2,200 county medical societies; 1,000 educational societies of one kind or another; and some 12,000 local trade associations.

Efforts to affect public attitudes today need not be haphazard. They rest on a solid basis of accumulated knowledge—the result of decades of study, research, and field work in the social sciences. The individual and the mass mind have been explored. Individual and social psychology, economics, sociology, politics, and government have provided a background of information for those engaged in adult education.

In our complex twentieth-century civilization, the dissemination of ideas has been accelerated through technological improvements and other elements. Today literacy is widespread. Some of it may be only surface literacy, but with the radio added, it furnishes audiences of millions upon millions of men and women. Ideas and opinions expressed in one place reach, practically instantaneously, throughout the whole world. That makes it incumbent on the believers in democracy to make use of the channels open to all. Only in this way can democracy hope to survive.

IMPORTANCE OF PRIVATE ENTERPRISE

Let me give you an example of a specific idea which, it seems to me, it is important to project at this time if we would preserve democracy. Millions have no concept of its significance. It is important for the public to understand and accept the vital part which private enterprise has played and is playing in preserving democracy. Private enterprise serves to preserve democracy.

Let me explain why. In the United States and in many parts of the world today there is a definite drift towards state capitalism— towards the control of private enterprise by the state. The very nature of a democracy is that it shall have checks and balances, that it shall take into consideration opposing viewpoints, that it shall not be authoritarian. But the very nature of our economic system demands that it shall be handled with the greatest speed of action.

A drift towards state capitalism must therefore bring in its train a greater concentration of power on the part of government. A greater concentration of power might place limitations on the checks and balances of a democratic system, might lead to the breaking down of the safeguards of democracy—the freedom of opinion, of speech, of the press, of assembly, of petition, of religion.

LINKING PRIVATE ENTERPRISE WITH DEMOCRACY

The way to ward off state capitalism is to reestablish belief in free competition and private enterprise—inseparable parts of our present democratic system. Let me give one example of how such a revitalized belief in the present system of private enterprise and democracy might be built up: The New York World's Fair might be utilized to teach the millions of Americans who will visit it or hear of it, dramatically, graphically, effectively, how our democracy works, and what its values are, by injecting into the Fair the keynote of the relation of every aspect of American life to America's essential democratic system, by presenting exhibits in terms not of themselves alone but of their relation to the American system.

Thus, for example, an automobile can be presented in terms of its larger significance of democracy—in terms of the greater freedom of motion it offers to individuals and groups, at a cost within the reach of all income groups in the nation. Freedom of motion brings with it facilities for the freer exchange of ideas, a greater opportunity to see and experience how other groups in other localities live and meet their problems. This interchange of ideas and knowledge, brought about by more extensive, quicker, and cheaper transportation in any of its forms, thus becomes an educational force in bringing about closer understanding between different sections, different groups, different individuals. It becomes a conduit for democratic thought and ideas. The automobile can be shown, as well, in its relation to democracy—its contribution to taxes and the use made of them for the people. The automobile thus becomes more than a mechanism on wheels-it becomes an instrument of democracy.

PRESENTING DEMOCRACY'S VALUES

Today it behooves those who are interested in preserving democracy to teach, and to continue to teach, democracy's values so that the work and contributions of past and present generations in all fields may be consolidated and perpetuated.

It is a hopeful sign that the colleges and universities of the country are aware of the responsibility of leadership in democracy. In a survey conducted by the speaker in collaboration with Doris E. Fleischman, many leading institutions were found offering courses which give students an understanding of the essentials for presenting opinions and points of view. Only by presenting the democratic point of view effectively, and making it a vital part of the beliefs of our people, can democracy be preserved in these difficult times.

It is thus our duty to strengthen the program of public education and public information to the end that everyone in America may understand the social significance of democracy, and its value for every man, woman, and child. What we must strive for is achievement of that inner faith and devotion to democracy within our people which will make them active against encroachments on the essential liberties which are the basis of democracy.

Speak Up For Democracy
A Program Outlined for Patriots . . . Group Leaders . . . Believers in America

(1940)

MILLIONS OF AMERICANS ARE OUT OF SYMPATHY with American Democracy. Native-born or foreign-born, Communists, Nazis, Fascists or fellow-travelers, these millions are more sympathetic with the institutions and policies of Soviet Russia, Nazi Germany, or Fascist Italy than those of the United States.

The depression, stripping men of assets and opportunities, weakened belief in democracy. Since them the military machines and dynamic propaganda of Communists, Fascists and Nazis have vanquished democracy in most of Europe and placed it squarely on the defensive its last great stronghold, the United States.

I admit that democracy is on the defensive in the United States. I propose that it be defended. By constructing vast fighting forces, land, sea and air! That, of course—but that is only part of the proposal. In large degree, the strength of our fighting forces will depend on the depth and breadth of our belief in our institutions. "Armies fight as the people think," a wise British general noted. To widen and deepen our beliefs in our institutions, I propose that all of us, our leaders as well as our rank and file, become propagandists for democracy.

"Speak up for democracy"—my message boils down to four words.

This program is not academic, not visionary. It is realistic, tangible. It applies proved methods of persuasion, of influencing, crystallizing and mobilizing public opinion. The mobilization of public opinion has been my profession and avocation for more than twenty-five years. My wife and I first called our joint work "counsel on public relations" eighteen years ago. In all modesty, may I say that my counsel has been sought and applied by many of America's greatest corporations, by highly placed individuals, by government. And so I ask for credence when I say that the program here suggested will work.

The billions of dollars being spent for national defense will be uselessly spent unless, throughout the country, there is a fundamental belief in and reliance upon democracy. Ignorance or rejection of the worth of democracy is a greater menace to his country than any "fifth column," than any foreign army or navy.

Now, how shall we go about revitalizing democracy—the whole of democracy for all the people? Men and women want to contribute something more personal to democracy than a few dollars or the use of their name on some organization's letterhead. And they can. The way to save democracy is to go out and save it. And the way to do that is for everyone to *mold public opinion for democracy to the limit of his own power*.

In the United States, there are thousands of professional molders of public opinion in politics, business and other fields—newspaper and magazine men, writers, scenarists, radio commentators, others. All can do their part in fighting for democracy. They do not need to be told how. They know. But in time of peril the United States does not entrust its defense to the professional solider alone. Like the protection of the country militarily, its protection ideologically depends on the aggressive activity of all—and ideas are as valuable in defense as armaments.

The molding of public opinion for democracy must not come only from the top, from Roosevelts and Willkies. Members of every group of society must assume responsibilities—and the value of democracy must be directly related to the individuals in that group.

"I like the American Way," an Eastern manufacturer said recently. "Why?"

"Because my mail reaches me as it was sent—uncensored. No one taps my telephone. I can join any political party I wish. I can vote for what and whom I please. I can read, see and hear what I choose. I can express opinions openly, even when they are 'agin' government men and measures."

That statement dealt with abstractions—liberty, justice, rights— but they meant much to that American. They will mean as much to other Americans who think their meanings through. But there are people in this country who have thought no further than did many in Germany, when the Nazis were getting under way. They wanted to protect their property, as who doesn't? They gave money to a political leader named Hitler who excoriated democracy and promised them that their property would be secure. The rest they now know too well.

Many here also fail to recognize the good fortune they enjoy under democracy, the misfortune that would come to them if democracy were to be displaced by Nazism, Fascism or Communism. Young college graduates, taxicab drivers, professional men—all sorts of people—go far astray.

A Harvard professor recently told me that, after a long lecture he had given to his class on democracy, one of his students said: "It's all hokum, but I believe it anyway." He really had no realization of what democracy meant to him.

Another college graduate I know, a young woman, feels that her country is a failure because it has not given her and the young man she wants to marry security for life. To her, all else is unimportant. She is interested only in a Utopian United States.

A taxicab driver, during a national political convention this year, took a good deal of his time and mine to belittle democratic processes. The convention delegation, he was sure, were interested solely in "women and the bottle," and so "a dictator would be a hell of lot better." That taxicab driver should be taught how subjects are treated in dictator countries.

A professional man I know told me with chuckle-headed cheerfulness of a manufacturing concern in which he has an interest: "We aren't going to take war contracts. Why should we be stuck with them? While our competitors are loading up with war contracts on a cost-plus basis, we'll be doing a bang-up business in regular directions." It never occurred to him to identify himself with the government and the national defense in this regard.

The cure for these misapprehensions in our democracy is, I believe, more democracy. In a dictatorship, propaganda is a function of the state. In a democracy it must be a function of the people. So the program I propose falls into two fields. One would be cultivated by the leaders of every kind of group—social, educational, neighborhood, religious, athletic, and so on. The other would be cultivated by men and women of all sorts everywhere at all times.

Many different kinds of groups function in the United States, and each has its group leaders, its molder of opinion. Each leader influences his constituents on matters of direct concern to his group. But he has influence extending beyond that particular subject. Realizing this, he should strive to become more articulate regarding democracy, more efficient as a molder of public opinion in its favor.

Molding public opinion is not a gift or an inspiration. Like other professions—law, engineering, architecture—it combines a science and an art. It applies established principles of psychology, sociology and other social sciences to the achievement of definite goals. It is up to our group leaders to study these principles and learn how they can be used to mold public opinion for democracy.

The average group leader may be in a better position to do this than average group members. There are courses, at universities and elsewhere, in which the subject is taught. There are books on public opinion in libraries. To find them consult *A Reference Guide to Public Opinion*, issued by the Princeton University Press. Good books to start with are Walter Lippman's *Public Opinion* and Peter Odegard's *The American Public Mind*. The author of this article has written *Propaganda* and *Crystallizing Public Opinion*.

To mold public opinion, the group leader must know what governs public actions; must understand the groups that make up society; must have a feeling for the value and effect of words and pictures. He must know the media through which facts and opinions are brought to the people in his community. When he does know, he can meet with effective counter-propaganda all attacks on democracy.

The great instruments—the press, the radio, the motion picture, the school, the lecture platform—that mold public opinion in his community are open to the group leader if he brings them the ideas and material their publics demand. He should make a study of their activities and needs. He should know what constituencies the ideas the newspapers in his city represent; what their policies are in news and editorial coverage; who the editors are; and on what basis they desire news referring to the activities for democracy he may set in motion.

He should be acquainted, also, with the policies and personnel of the radio stations and press services in his territory. He should know the character and location of any public forum in his community. He should know who books the important speaking engagements in his town and why and where. He should know who in his community represents the leading newsreel companies.

With these facts before him he can plan his campaign for democracy in terms of the kind of material these media carry. If he finds leaders of other groups in his town who are of the same mind, together they can organize a joint executive committee to work for the common goal.

And every group member, as well as group leader, can do his part in selling democracy. If you believe in democracy, say so. If you understand its magnificent realities as they affect the individual's day to day life, stress them. Affirm the truth. Scratch the lie. All of us can be champions of democracy within our own sphere—to our friends and families, to the people we meet, to the butcher, baker, candlestick maker.

The most common accusations against democracy number less than a dozen. Each of us can have available strong and truthful answers to them, and help bury the accusations by incessant repetition of the answers.

Here is a list of the common accusations against democracy in the United States:

1. Democratic processes are too slow, too inefficient.

   Answer: Democratic processes are planned to provide for full, free discussion, which takes time. Thus decisions can be reached between conflicting points of view, giving the greatest satisfaction to the greatest number. Normally, process in our democracy comes the safe, lasting way, through evolutionary change. But we have often risen to an emergency—note the speed with which Congress enacted recovery legislation in 1933 and defense legislation in 1940. In such cases it has shown all the force and speed of the autocracies, without their abuse of power.

2. Freedom of speech is a meaningless freedom except for the man wo acts as if it were license. Then it should be forbidden.

   Answer: Have you ever criticized this government, or specifically Mr. Roosevelt? How would you like to be sent to a concentration camp for doing so? That is what happens to you for criticizing the government in a dictatorship. The basic purpose of freedom of speech, and of the press, and of assembly, is to facilitate human communication, to enable the people, by free interchange of ideas, to arrive at sound conclusions leading to intelligent action. As Lyman

Bryson, distinguished American educator, puts it, "If every man can say what he pleases, we have a fair chance at getting at the truth." If this freedom is meaningless, truth itself is meaningless. And so is rational action.

3. Security in a dictatorship is more important than liberty in a democracy.

Answer: Liberty and security are not mutually exclusive—that is totalitarian propaganda. The greatest degree of economic security known on this earth was known in the Scandinavian democracies recently destroyed by Communism and Fascism. And they also enjoyed great liberty. In a dictatorship, on the other hand, there is no real security—not even security of life. Many of Hitler's good friends would testify to the fact had they not been murdered in the blood purge of 1934 or later.

4. Dictatorships are superior to democracy because they have eliminated unemployment.

Answer: The alternative we face is not "no job under democracy" vs. "job under dictatorship." We Americans are striving constantly to combat unemployment, as our C.C.C., W.P.A, and other government projects indicate. Dictatorships, meanwhile, strive to create not the fact but the illusion that, under their systems, everyone has a job. In a dictatorship, everyone is actually or potentially part of a system of forced labor—tomorrow the expert accountant may be made to slaughter hogs; tomorrow the Montana cowboy may be forced to dig Bronx sewers. The right to strike is forfeit; the right to bargain is unknown. The activity in which, under dictatorship, labor shares is largely activity in preparation for war. In the U.S., labor is still free—to organize, to bargain collectively, to quit and take another job. Meanwhile, M.E. Tracy, former editor of *Current History*, phrases it neatly: "Nazism, Communism and Fascism boast of the fact that they have no unemployment. Neither does a prison nor an army."

5. Most people are too ignorant and stupid to vote intelligently, as under democracy they should.

    Answer: Abraham Lincoln said, "No man is good enough to govern any other man without that other's consent." Those who accuse the majority of stupidity rarely class themselves among the majority. The real alternatives here are majority rule vs. dictator rule. In a democracy there are always opportunities under intelligent leadership for peaceful conversion of a venal, despotic or stupid majority opinion. Thomas Jefferson wrote: "I know of no safe depository of the ultimate powers of society but the people themselves; and if we think them not enlightened enough to exercise their control with a wholesome discretion, the remedy is not to take it from them, but to inform their discretion by education." If a dictator has anti-social qualities—and also the 600,000 police supposedly in Hitler's Gestapo—what is to be done?

6. Gangsterism in this country shows that our democracy has rotted, and must be superseded by a stronger system like Fascism or Communism.

    Answer: Here the gangsters are illegal. In dictator countries, the gangsters are legal. They are the government and the law. When the people of this country are sufficiently aroused, they invoke the law and gangsters are eliminated. In dictator nations only a bloody revolution can shake the gangsters from their hold.

7. Democracy has representative government, not democratic government. The men who govern act according to their constituents' desires. Their actions are not necessarily in the public interest. They are actions predicated on the self-interest of the individual legislator and of his group. How much better would be the decision reached by a strong man at the top!

   Answer: This is presupposed that the strong man knows, and always acts on, the right answer. It is taking a much greater chance to place your trust in one man than in the self-interest of many groups. Occasionally, benevolent despots arise. History quickly points out how very few there have ever been.

8. As science and invention continue, there will be less opportunity for the democratic state to function though its electorate. The best method for carrying on government activities will have been determined. And in a dictatorship the Fuehrer can quickly avail himself of all the findings of science and invention without having to convince the people of their validity.

   Answer: How can we be sure that the dictator has the all-seeing wisdom to make only sound and scientific decisions? When he is wrong, his decisions carry the same force and weight as when he is right. The "scientific" blood theories of the Nazis have been disproved, and yet carry the weight of truth in Nazi Germany. Is it not better to let the people absorb truth and science more slowly than to let all suffer from someone's crackpot pseudo-scientific notions?

The refugees who have come to us from dictatorship countries give a picture that the individual who lives here can hardly comprehend. Whenever the house doorbell rang, they were in mortal fear that it might be the Gestapo or its equivalent. When they walked along the street and were eyed by a casual stranger, they were afraid of being picked up and never heard from again. When the children did not come home exactly at the appointed hour, who knew but that they might have been apprehended? No telephone conversation was safe. Every activity was at the whim of an impersonal and arbitrary power.

Do we want that kind of life in these United States of America? You know we don't. Let's not have it. Let's speak up for our United States, our America, our democracy—now!

CREDITS

"Manipulating Public Opinion: The Why and the How." *American Journal of Sociology*, Volume 33, Issue 6 (May 1928): 958–71. Reprinted with permission of University of Chicago Press Journals, permission conveyed through Copyright Clearance Center, Inc.

"The Engineering of Consent." *The Annals of the American Academy of Political and Social Science*, Volume: 250 Issue 1 (March 1, 1947): 113–20. Reprinted with permission of Sage Publications, permission conveyed through Copyright Clearance Center, Inc.

"Molding Public Opinion." *The Annals of the American Academy of Political and Social Science*, Vol. 179, Pressure Groups and Propaganda (May 1935): 82–87. Reprinted with permission of Sage Publications, permission conveyed through Copyright Clearance Center, Inc.

"Attitude Polls-Servants or Masters?" *The Public Opinion Quarterly*, Vol. 9, No. 3 (Autumn 1945): 264. Reprinted with permission of Oxford University Press, permission conveyed through Copyright Clearance Center, Inc.

"Chapter II: The New Propaganda." *Propaganda* (1928; reis., Brooklyn: Ig Publishing, 2005).

"Why We Behave Like Inhuman Beiings," *Household*, (February 1949): 69–76.

"An Educational Program for Unions" *ILR Review*, Vol. 1, No. 1 (October 1947): 103–9. Reprinted with permission of Sage Publications, permission conveyed through Copyright Clearance Center, Inc.

"Human Engineering and Social Adjustment" *ETC: A Review of General Semantics*, Vol. 36, No. 2 (Summer 1979):198–203. Reprinted with permission of the Institute of General Semantics.

"The Public Relations Counsel; the Increased and Increasing Importance of the Profession"; "What Constitutes Public Opinion?"; "Is Public Opinion Stubborn or Malleable?"; "The Interaction of Public Opinion with the Forces that Help to Make It"; and "The Power of Interacting Forces that Go to Make Up Public Opinion." *Crystallizing Public Opinion* (1923; reis., Brooklyn: Ig Publishing, 2011).

"Emergence of the Public Relations Counsel: Principles and Recollections." *The Business History Review*, Vol. 45, No. 3 (Autumn 1971): 296–316. Reprinted with permission of Cambridge University Press.

"The Marketing of National Policies: A Study of War Propaganda." *Journal of Marketing*, Vol. 6, No. 3 (January 1942): 236–244. Reprinted with permission of Sage Publications, permission conveyed through Copyright Clearance Center, Inc.

"The Press Must Act to Meet Postwar Responsibility." *Journalism Quarterly*, Volume 21, Issue 2 (June 1, 1944):122–29.

"Public Education for Democracy." *The Annals of the American Academy of Political and Social Science*, Vol. 198, Present International Tensions (July 1938): 124–27. Reprinted with permission of Sage Publications, permission conveyed through Copyright Clearance Center.

"Speak Up for Democracy" *Current History & Forum*, Vol. 52, No. 2 (October 22, 1940): 21–24.